GÉRARD PIOUFFRE

First Class

Legendary Ocean Liner Voyages
Around the World

THE VENDOME PRESS

NEW YORK

Contents

Introduction   9

The Mediterranean and the Suez Canal   49

The Transatlantic Crossing and the Blue Riband   97

The South Atlantic and Caribbean   153

Through the Suez Canal to the Far East   201

The Transpacific Crossing   257

Routes of Ice and Gold   305

Index   353

Citations   357

Bibliography   358

Photo Credits   359

Acknowledgements   340

1 | An ocean liner steams onward to a distant port.

2 | The second SS *France* in a detail of a 1912 poster by Albert Sébille.

4 | Bidding farewell to the *Empress of Scotland,* c.1920.

6–7 | First-class passengers flank the captain of the Royal Mail Steam Packet Company's *Orca*, July 26, 1925.

7

8 | The Cunard Line's celebrated *Mauretania*, several times winner of the Blue Riband.

9 | A Polish immigrant arriving at Ellis Island, c.1910.

INTRODUCTION

At a time when air travel has become so much a part of life, it is difficult to conceive that until quite recently the only way of crossing the world's oceans was by boat. Until the mid-nineteenth century, the great navigation routes were the preserve of sailing ships: even with the dependable trade winds, voyages took an eternity. In the early nineteenth century a ship had to allow seven or eight weeks for the Atlantic crossing, and up to twice as long if the ship was either becalmed or caught up in bad weather.

In 1817, five American ship-owners got together to establish a regular link between New York and Liverpool. Carrying letters and small packets for urgent delivery, the four sailing boats they had built for the Black Ball Line were known as packet boats. As mail was not a bulky cargo, it left room on every crossing for a few passengers. Few in number though they were initially, these passengers nevertheless represented an appreciable supplementary income. Thus as the number of shipping companies multiplied, so they vied with each for the passenger trade.

From 1840, the Old World began to realize that it had too many mouths to feed, while the New World lacked manpower. Immigration to the United States and Canada assumed new proportions, and over the next decade some

9

two million people left Europe to seek their fortune in the Americas. The ships on which these families crossed the Atlantic still had masts and sails, but now these were only a secondary means of propulsion. The great novelty was the steam engine. The French inventor Denis Papin had done pioneering work on an early version in 1707. In Britain, Patrick Miller, James Taylor, and William Symington, and above all Thomas Newcomen and James Watt, went on to develop the steam engine that would pave the way for the Industrial Revolution. In America, John Fitch adapted James Watt's steam engine to power small boats. These experiments proved so promising that in 1807 Robert Fulton succeeded in using a James Watt steam engine to power a larger vessel, the *Clermont*, with which he launched a commercial service between Albany and New York.

The *Clermont* proved an instant success, and in the months that followed numerous other steamers began to

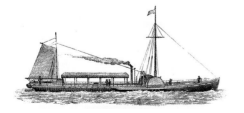

ply the rivers and lakes of North America. They were propelled by paddle wheels, which made them easy to maneuver and particularly well suited to river navigation. On the high seas, by contrast, the system proved too fragile, and accidents caused by paddle wheels running out of control in heavy swells were numerous.

The answer to the problem was to come in the form of the propeller. The device had been known since the Renaissance, when it appeared in several of Leonardo da Vinci's sketches. But no practical use for it was discovered until the early nineteenth century when the experiments of Austrian Josef Ressel and Frenchman Frédéric Sauvage led to the idea of a screw propeller for ships. By the 1840s, the steamships *Robert F. Stockton* and *Archimedes* were equipped with propellers attached to shafts. But the metal shafts were naturally rigid, proving incompatible with the more flexible timber of contemporary ship hulls. Accidents were commonplace, until advances in metallurgy meant that hulls could be built of iron, and later of steel. Metal hulls could also be of much greater length than wooden ones, which could not safely exceed 200 feet (approximately 60 meters). The new metal steamships grew ever bigger, faster, and more luxurious. The first

10 | The *Clermont*, Robert Fulton's large river paddle steamer, which sailed between Albany and New York.

11 | Launched in 1837, Isambard Kingdom Brunel's *Great Western* was the world's largest steamship. In her nine years of service, between 1838 and 1847, she made 67 Atlantic crossings.

12 | Brunel's hugely ambitious iron steamship the *Great Eastern.* Shortly after her 1858 launch, Jules Verne mocked the vessel as "20,000 tons of vanity," but he sailed to America on her in 1867 and made her the setting of his novel *A Floating City.*

13 | Keeping the roaring furnaces stoked on a steam-powered vessel was a difficult and dangerous job that entailed shoveling massive quantities of coal and white-hot ash in temperatures of up to 112°F (45°C), with the constant risk of potentially fatal blow-backs. This image from William Whitelock Lloyd's *P&O Pencillings* shows stokers at work on the SS *Himalaya* in the early 1890s.

revolutionary steamers were Isambard Kingdom Brunel's *Great Britain* (1843) at 322 feet (98 meters), the first ship made of metal, powered by an engine and driven by a propeller; and above all the *Great Eastern* (1852), at almost 700 feet (213 meters). This leviathan was capable of carrying more than 4,000 passengers and inspired Jules Verne's novel *A Floating City.*

From 1845 the great steamship came of age—at once a ship, an industrial plant, and a floating hotel complex. The sailors who navigated them were heirs to a long tradition; they had grown up in the age of sail, when they had developed their navigation skills to the fullest. Now they viewed the passing of that age with regret. The wind that used to fill their ships' sails had been replaced by an industrial plant run by specialists and employing an unqualified workforce. The former often came from the railway companies; the latter's job was to keep the engines stoked and distribute the coal among the ships' holds. Muscle power was all that was necessary.

As it grew into the ocean liner, the steamship also became a complex of hotels, complete with rooms, restaurants, and entertainment. Hotels in the plural because, in reality, there were as many distinct hotels as

there were classes on a boat. Looking after the passengers' needs required an army of specialists whose skills had little to do with the world of seamanship, including chambermaids, stewards and stewardesses, bellboys, chefs, musicians, and sports instructors. The shipping companies employed some members of the hotel staff; others were supplied by a whole range of subcontractors. Transporting mail was still highly profitable, and some British steam packets proudly sported the letters RMS, standing for Royal Mail Steamer, in front of their names. From the late nineteenth century, however, passenger

14 | The galleys on this Norddeutscher Lloyd liner were equipped to provide three meals a day for passengers in all three classes. The Luggage label is from the Norddeutscher Lloyd liner *Coblenz*, which sailed on Far Eastern routes. This owner of this luggage disembarked at Belawan in Sumatra, Indonesia.

15 | Only the portholes betray the fact that this hairdressing salon is on board the Messageries Maritimes liner *Champollion* and not on terra firma.

NORDDEUTSCHER LLOYD

Coblenz

Belawan

ZIMMER - STATEROOM

15

transport became the shipping lines' principal source of revenue, well ahead of cargo and even of mail.

In 1894, the British engineer Sir Charles Parsons built a small boat powered by a steam turbine of his own invention. The *Turbinia* made a spectacular unauthorized public debut at the Spithead Naval Review of 1897, part of Queen Victoria's Diamond Jubilee, when it slalomed at unprecedented speeds of up to 34.5 knots between the warships of the greatest armada the world had ever seen, even as Navy picket boats attempted to stop it. Four years later, the Allan Line fitted Parsons turbines to its transatlantic steamships RMS *Victorian* and RMS *Virginian*.

The great ocean liners now had a means of propulsion of a power to match their size: after trials with a Parsons turbine on the Carmania of 1905, Cunard fitted them to its great *Mauretania* and *Lusitania*.

At this period, passengers were divided into three classes. Most numerous were the immigrants, who traveled in third class. These were the passengers on whom the shipping lines depended for their livelihood, and they spared no pains in their efforts to attract them.

Passengers in second class were generally traveling for professional reasons, consisting largely of army officers or colonial administrators going on leave or returning to their postings, merchants, traders, and wealthy tourists. An extremely profitable clientele, they were also of great interest to the shipping companies.

But the passengers who were the showcase for the shipping lines were those in first class, the barons of the worlds of finance, commerce, and industry. Although they were the least profitable of all, by reason of the sheer numbers of hotel personnel needed to attend to them, nothing was felt to be too good for them.

The advertising campaigns undertaken by the shipping lines rested on the services they offered. In this

16 | With her sister ship the *Mauretania*, the *Lusitania* snatched the Blue Riband from their German rivals. On May 7, 1915, the *Lusitania* was torpedoed and sunk by the U-boat U-20, under the command of Kapitän-leutnant Walther Schwieger, with the loss of 1198 lives, including 128 Americans. Condemned as a war crime by the British press, this disaster was to influence America's entry into the war in April 1917.

17 | The arrival of the liner *Eugène-Péreire* (1888–1929) at Algiers was a major event, attracting an excited crowd. On her maiden voyage, this liner completed the journey from Marseille to Algiers in a record 24 hours.

18 | Ships may have only ladders, but this sweeping descent on board the *König Albert* of the Norddeutscher Lloyd Line was so far removed from a ship's ladder that even the ship's crew had no hesitation in calling it a staircase.

19 | The grand staircase on RMS *Olympic* of the White Star Line. On the landing is the clock depicting *Honor and Glory Crowning Time*. The *Titanic* had the same clock on its grand staircase. Both staircases were intended only for use by first-class passengers.

golden age of the ocean liner, the greatest interior designers vied with each other to transform the great ships into authentic floating palaces. This was the era of classical decoration and skilful pastiche. Thus the *Amerika*, owned by the German shipping line Hapag, had interior designs by the distinguished architect Charles Mewès, who also designed the interiors of the *Kaiserin Auguste Victoria*. For the decoration of the *Lusitania* and *Mauretania*, the Cunard directors called on the talents of

two other famous architects, James Miller and Harold Peto. Cunard's rivals, the White Star Line, meanwhile, entrusted the decoration of the *Olympic* and the *Titanic* to Alexander Carlisle, head designer for the Irish shipyard Harland and Wolff. As a general rule good taste prevailed, even if passengers might have felt they were in a chateau rather than on board ship.

The arrangements for passengers in second class were not quite as luxurious, but they nevertheless enjoyed the use of immense drawing rooms and dining rooms, libraries, and smoking rooms. Here again, the designers were at pains to encourage passengers to forget entirely that they were at sea. On most liners, second class imitated the style of a large and impressively appointed country house.

Nor were passengers traveling in third class overlooked. Cabins might be shared, on the dormitory principle, but the dark, airless steerage of the steam packets was now only a distant memory. Henceforth third class accommodation was plain but comfortable.

In the early years of the twentieth century, ocean liners belonging to shipping companies from all the great sea powers plied the world's oceans. Britain occupied a dominant position, its vast empire offering valuable colonial

20 | The Viennese café on board the Norddeutscher Lloyd steam packet *Kaiser Wilhelm II*, was designed by the interior designer Johannes Poppe as a cosy, comfortable space—despite the heavy neo-baroque decorations in vogue at the turn of the twentieth century.

21 | Even the most jaded of first-class passengers could hardly have remained unimpressed by the dining room on board the Norddeutscher Lloyd liner *Kronprinz Wilhelm* (shown here in its full splendor, c.1900), with the magnificent carved-stucco paneling and green silk hangings, and the elaborately carved and gilded staircase.

outlets to its major shipping lines, Cunard, White Star, and the Peninsular & Oriental Steam Navigation Company, better known as the P&O. Cunard came into existence in 1840 as the British and North American Royal Mail Steam-Packet Company. Renamed the Cunard Steamship Company Limited in 1879, it operated mainly in the North Atlantic, where it rapidly gained a reputation for solid dependability. The company was at the height of its powers in 1906, when it launched the superliners *Mauretania* and *Lusitania*, soon dubbed the "Cunard greyhounds."

Cunard's great rival in the North Atlantic was the White Star Line, formed in 1845 as the White Star Line of Boston Packets. Declared bankrupt in 1868, it was taken over by Thomas Ismay, and, like Cunard, reached its zenith in the years before the outbreak of World War I, when it launched the *Olympic*, followed by the *Titanic* and the *Gigantic*, the latter renamed the *Britannic* before she was launched. The moment she came into service, the *Olympic* eclipsed all other existing liners in her sheer size and the opulence of her appointments. Even more glorious was the *Titanic,* which tragically hit an iceberg and sank on her maiden voyage. This disaster, in which 1500 lives were lost, considerably weakened White Star, which was absorbed by

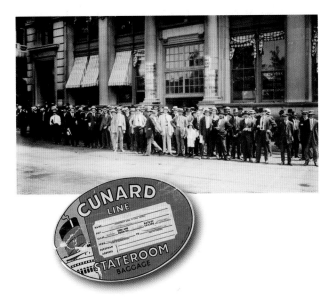

23

24–5 | All the great shipping lines had their own facilities in the United States. Taken in November 1914, this photograph shows Norddeutscher Lloyd's Pier 2 on the Hudson River in Hoboken, New Jersey.

PIER No 2

ORTH GERMAN LLOYD

GERMAN

25

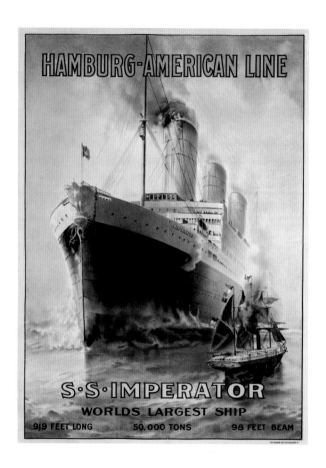

the Royal Mail Steam Packet Company in 1926, itself taken over by Cunard in 1934.

In the Hamburg-Amerikanische Packetfahrt Actien-Gesellschaft (Hapag), Germany possessed the most powerful shipping company in continental Europe. In the early twentieth century it operated some of the world's most splendid ocean liners, and when Cunard launched the *Mauretania* and the *Lusitania*, Hapag responded with its Big Three: *Imperator, Vaterland* and *Bismarck*.

Like Britain and Germany, France before World War I possessed an immense colonial empire. The Compagnie Générale Transatlantique, founded by the Pereire brothers in 1855 as the Compagnie Générale Maritime, assured links between metropolitan France and the colonies. In the years leading up to the war, the company served chiefly the West Indies and the New York route. The other main French shipping line was the Compagnie des Messageries Maritimes, which served Cochin China, Indochina, the Indian Ocean, Australia, and the Mediterranean ports. Other French companies operated regular services to Africa, the Mediterranean, South America, and the Far East. The largest of these were the Compagnie des Chargeurs Réunis, the Compagnie Fraissinet Fabre, the

26 | A Hamburg-American Line (Hapag) poster depicting the liner *Imperator*, "the world's largest ship." When Cunard announced that its *Aquitania* would be a foot (30cm) longer, Hapag countered by endowing the *Imperator* with a figurehead consisting of an eagle with outspread wings clutching a globe in its talons, increasing the overall length of the vessel to 919 feet (280 meters), some 9 feet (3 meters) longer than the Aquitania.

27 | Poster showing the Hapag liner *Deutschland*, several times winner of the Blue Riband, c.1901.

Hamburg Amerika

27

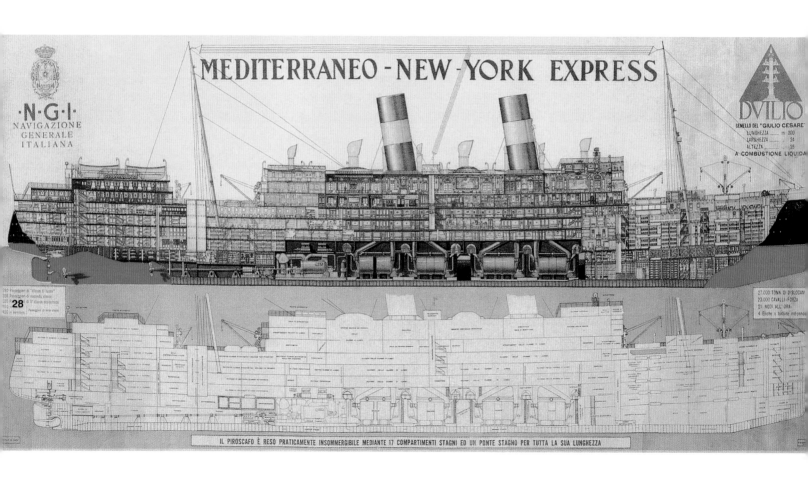

MEDITERRANEO - NEW - YORK EXPRESS

· N·G·I ·
NAVIGAZIONE
GENERALE
ITALIANA

DVILIO
GEMELLO DEL "GIULIO CESARE"
LUNGHEZZA ___ m 200
LARGHEZZA ___ 24
ALTEZZA ___ 25
A COMBUSTIONE LIQUIDA

28

IL PIROSCAFO È RESO PRATICAMENTE INSOMMERGIBILE MEDIANTE 17 COMPARTIMENTI STAGNI ED UN PONTE STAGNO PER TUTTA LA SUA LUNGHEZZA

28 | Longitudinal cross-section through the Navigazione Generale Italiana (NGI) liner *Duilio*, launched in October 1923. Built for the Naples–New York route, she was transferred to the Genoa–Buenos Aires route in 1928. She was sunk by Allied aerial action in July 1944.

29 | RMS *Olympic* of the White Star Line, the lead ship in the class that also included the *Titanic* and the *Gigantic*. Contrary to popular belief, none of this trio of leviathans was designed specifically to win the Blue Riband. The label is from Cunard White Star Line.

Compagnie Paquet, and the Société Générale des Transports Maritimes (SGTM).

A Spanish presence on the high seas was assured by the Compañía Trasatlántica Española, with routes chiefly to Cuba and South America. Italy had a number of shipping lines, the largest being the Compagnia di Navigazione Generale Italiana, formed from a merger of the Florio and Rubattino companies, which served the Mediterranean and the Atlantic routes.

Before World War I, America was represented widely if indirectly on the world's shipping routes, through the major financial institutions that controlled numerous European shipping lines. The most famous of these was built on the multimillion-dollar fortune of John Pierpont Morgan, owner of J.P. Morgan and Company, one of the largest and most powerful banking institutions in the world. Through skillful mergers and takeovers between his numerous financial and industrial concerns, Morgan controlled the United States Steel Corporation and the major American railroad companies, as well as becoming the major shareholder of the shipping line International Mercantile Marine (IMM). From its headquarters in New Jersey, IMM was the owner of the American Line, the Red

WHITE STAR LINE
TRIPLE SCREW STEAMER
882½ FT. LONG   "OLYMPIC"   46,359 TONS

29

Star Line, the Atlantic Transport Line, and the National Line, and was the majority shareholder in the Leyland Line. IMM also controlled the International Navigation Company, which in turn owned the Oceanic Steam Navigation Company, itself the sole shareholder in the White Star Line. On top of all this, the International Navigation Company was the proprietor of the British & North Atlantic Steam Navigation Company and the Mississippi & Dominion Steamship Company. John Pierpont Morgan thus enjoyed direct control over the cream of British shipping lines, and—through his banks—a major interest in a number of European naval shipyards.

The modest shipyards that had previously specialized in timber construction had by now disappeared or been converted to building in metal. In the age of the ocean liners, shipbuilding became the preserve of engineers, and it was they who ruled over the drafting departments. Every element, every detail of the great liners was the object of meticulous plans: in the end, several thousand plans, drawings, and sketches would be submitted to the shipbuilders who would carry out the construction. The first step was the laying of the keel on wooden piles known as tins. Then the timber structure was added and faced with

30 | The great Hapag liner *Vaterland*, launched on April 3, 1913, boasted a double hull intended as an extra safety feature. Seized by the United States government in 1917 for use as a troop ship during World War I, she was renamed *Leviathan*.

31 | SS *Aquitania*, launched by Cunard in May 1914, in dry dock, with the full expanse of her 899-foot (274-meter) hull exposed.

31

metal sheets designed to ensure the hull was watertight. These metal sheets were assembled by the use of thousands of rivets, heated until they were red hot and then inserted in the holes prepared to receive them. While one worker held the head with pliers, another would hammer the projecting tail of the shaft. As the rivets cooled, they held the sheets together with considerable force. Before the technique was developed for soldering sheets together, riveting was the only available method for metal-hull construction, and is thus found on all metal ships dating from the late nineteenth and early twentieth century. Indeed, rivets may be viewed as the signature of the age's engineers.

In order not to bring their enormous weight to bear on the slipway, the liners were always launched with the minimum of fittings and finished while afloat. The hull would then be besieged by an army of ironworkers, mechanics, electricians, plumbers, carpenters, cabinetmakers, painters, upholsterers, and more. In all, an ocean liner would require a workforce of some 10–15,000 men.

With its industrial might, Britain led the way, with the Elswick shipbuilding yard in Newcastle upon Tyne; Vickers in Barrow-in-Furness; Swan Hunter & Wigham Richardson in Wallsend, Tyne and Wear; John Brown in Clydebank; Fairfield Shipbuilding and Engineering in Glasgow; Yarrow in Scotstown; and Harland & Wolff in Belfast.

Germany possessed several major shipyards, most of them on its North Sea coastline. The largest was Blohm & Voss of Hamburg, followed by the two Vulkan yards, also in Hamburg, while Bremen had the Bremer Vulkan-Vegesack and Weser yards. The principal German ports on the Baltic also had smaller yards.

In France, merchant ships were built at the Ateliers et Chantiers de Bretagne in Nantes, at the Forges et Chantiers de la Gironde in Bordeaux, and at the Forges et Chantiers de la Méditerranée in La Seyne. Italy had yards at Genoa, Ancona, Muggiano in La Spezia, and Marghera. Although these yards did not build giant liners to rival those of the British and German yards, they nonetheless enjoyed an excellent reputation.

Every shipyard had dry docks, narrow pens or basins constructed alongside the river or sea so that vessels could be floated in at high tide. Left high and dry when the tide went out, they would then be shored up with wooden piles to keep them stable. At low tide, the entrance gates would be shut and any remaining water pumped out. In this way it was possible to work on parts of the ship that would

65 PULLMAN SLEEPERS WOULD BE NEEDED TO MOVE THE 2075 PASSENGERS WHICH THE "QUEEN MARY" CAN CARRY ON ONE TRIP ~ 15 COACHES WOULD BE NEEDED TO MOVE THE CREW,~ COMPARED TO.

The 200 PEOPLE THAT WERE PASSENGERS AND CREW ON THE FIRST CUNARDER "BRITANNIA"

normally be below the waterline; when the work was done, the gates would be opened at low tide so the vessel could float out again on the rising tide.

The ports of Europe and America were linked to major towns and cities by railways, and together trains and boats formed the fastest, most regular, and most reliable form of transport at this time. It comes as no surprise that when Jules Verne's hero Phileas Fogg embarked on his famous wager it never occurred to him to travel by any means except train and boat. The symbiotic relationship between the two was perfectly symbolized by the rise of the boat train: trains timetabled specifically to coincide with the arrival and departure of passenger liners. Thus central European railway services terminated at Hamburg or Bremen; the Mediterranean port of Brindisi was only a few hours by train from the major cities of Italy; and Southampton, England was a mere two hours from London's Waterloo Station. On the other side of the Channel, meanwhile, *transatlantique* trains provided a regular service between Paris and Le Havre or Cherbourg.

In the ports that attracted passengers in the largest numbers, the shipping lines built maritime stations (an inspiration for the architecture of present-day major airports) to house customs and immigration services, agencies for the shipping lines, shops for last-minute purchases, post offices, and foreign-exchange bureaus. The concept of travelling light was unknown before the mid-1950s, and armies of porters were employed to wheel mountains of trunks and cases on their barrows. In April 1912, for instance, Mrs. Charlotte Cardeza boarded the *Titanic* with fourteen steamer trunks, four suitcases, and three boxes. She was not an isolated case. Etiquette required that passengers in first and second class change

34 | Illustration showing the number of Pullman cars required to transport the passengers and crew of the RMS *Queen Mary*, launched on September 26, 1934: no fewer than 50 carriages to accommodate the 2075 passengers and a further 15 for the crew.

35 | In 1936, Naples built a vast new maritime railway station at Molo San Vicenzo. Conceived as a showcase for the modern Italian state, it reflected the grandiose Fascist program of the Italian dictator Benito Mussolini.

35

clothing at least three times daily, and there was naturally no question of a lady wearing the same outfit more than once during the crossing. The immigrants in third class could not afford such ostentation, but even their meager possessions would often fill several suitcases.

Passengers boarded ship by means of a gangplank, which might be covered or not, leading up to a gangway, an opening in the bulwark. The starboard (right) side of the ship was traditionally deemed smarter, and the shipping lines were consequently at pains to ensure that boarding took place on this side. When this was not

36–37 | The Norddeutscher Lloyd arrivals and departures hall in New York. The solicitous gentleman passenger may well be the sole owner of the mountain of portmanteaux, bags, boxes, and cases piled up on the trolley. At the arrival or departure of every passenger liner an army of porters would spring into action.

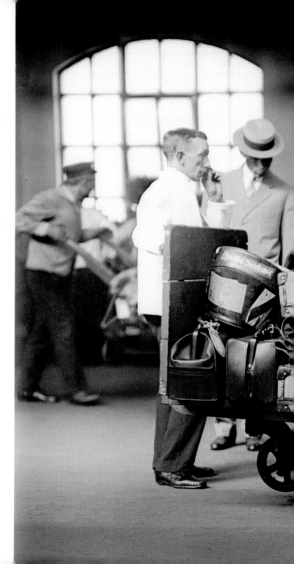

38 | In the early years of the twentieth century Cherbourg was a transatlantic port of major importance, but its harbor was not large enough to accommodate the great ocean liners. Small boats were therefore used to ferry passengers out to the liners as they lay at anchor. The ship shown here is a liner of the Norddeutscher Lloyd fleet, probably the *Ariadne*.

39 Top | Under a burning sun, families and onlookers gather on the Hapag pier in New York to wave off the *Imperator*.

39 Bottom | Passengers boarding the *Kaiser Wilhelm II* in New York.

possible, the ship's purser had to explain to passengers that boarding had to take place on the port side purely for technical reasons.

Some ports had not been designed to accommodate the massive liners of the North Atlantic lines. At New York it proved possible to enlarge the embarkation quays, but at Cherbourg and Queenstown the shipping companies had to use tenders, small vessels that carried passengers, luggage, and mail out to the great steamer while it lay at anchor in the harbor. At Cherbourg, third-class passengers of the White Star Line embarked with the mail and luggage on the *Traffic*, while passengers in first and second class began their journey on the *Nomadic*, a miniature version of an *Olympic*-series liner. Taken out of commission in 1969, the *Nomadic* was towed to Paris, where she was converted into a floating restaurant moored opposite the Eiffel Tower. In 2006 she returned to Belfast, her birthplace, where she is currently undergoing restoration with a view to putting her on display in 2012, to commemorate the centenary of the sinking of the *Titanic*.

During the World War I, the belligerent nations converted their ocean liners into troop carriers, hospital ships, or auxiliary battle cruisers. For many this was to

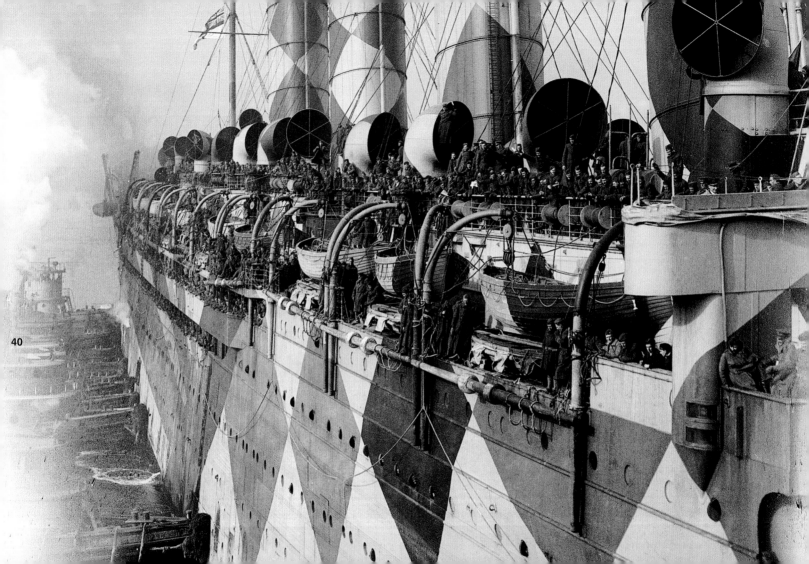

40 | As part of her conversion into a troop carrier during World War I, the Cunard liner *Mauretania* is here shown being painted with dazzle camouflage, consisting of geometrical shapes designed to prevent the enemy from accurately estimating her speed.

41 | "Avenge the *Lusitania*": this poster of 1915 urges Irishmen to join up in order to avenge the sinking of the *Lusitania* by a German U-boat, presented in the Allied press as a war crime.

prove their death knell. The White Star's *Britannic*, sister ship to the *Titanic*, was blown up by a German mine and sank in the straits of Kea (Tzia), south-east of Athens. The *Lusitania*, several times winner of the Blue Riband, was torpedoed by a German U-boat and sank off the coast of Ireland.

By the end of the war, the German Big Three liners were all in the hands of the victors. In 1917 the US Navy had seized the *Vaterland*, renamed *Leviathan* by her new peacetime owners, the United States Lines. Her two sister ships were handed over to the Allies as reparations at the end of hostilities: the *Imperator* went to Cunard and became the *Berengaria*, while the *Bismarck*, which had still been under construction at the beginning of the war, passed to the White Star Line as the *Majestic*. The White Star Line also inherited the *Columbus*, which it renamed the *Homeric*.

But the shipping lines quickly realized that making new things out of old was a costly activity, and from 1923 they set about building their fleets up again. With the *Île-de-France*, launched in 1926, the CGT scored a major success, but with the *Normandie* of 1932 they caused a sensation. Measuring 1,029 feet (313.6 meters) long and 119 feet (36.4 meters) wide, she was the largest ship ever built.

She was also universally agreed to be the most beautiful, and those who saw her tended to run out of superlatives with which to express their admiration.

In 1934, Cunard—now Cunard White Star, having taken over its rival—launched a great 88,000-ton superliner. The story goes that the company intended to call the ship the *Queen Victoria,* and duly asked George V's permission to name her after "Britain's greatest queen." He replied that he was sure his wife, Queen Mary, would be delighted. And so, in 1934, the *Queen Mary* was launched. On May 27, 1936 she set off on her maiden voyage to New York, and in the years that followed she and the *Normandie* vied with each other for the Blue Riband, until in 1938 she captured it definitively with a crossing of just three days, twenty hours, and forty-two minutes.

But it was not just on the North Atlantic crossing that new liners were introduced into service. Messageries Maritimes created a magnificently appointed series, all decorated in a style evoking the countries they served. P&O, meanwhile, built a series of 22,000-ton liners for routes to the Indies, Australia, and the Far East. On South American routes, Italy deployed the magnificent liners of the Italia Flotte Riunite, or Italian Line, and the Hamburg Südamerikanische was another major player. And Africa was well served by the British Union-Castle Line and the German Ost Afrika Linie.

The liners of the interwar years were very different from their predecessors, but—with their sloping keels, their aerodynamic lines, and their more modestly scaled funnels—perhaps just as elegant.

During World War II, as in I, ocean liners were pressed into service as troop carriers and auxiliary battle cruisers. They suffered heavy losses, but also indisputably shortened the war, as reiterated on several occasions by Cunard and by Winston Churchill.

After the end of the war, cruise liners became even more popular. As the world got back to work, people needed to travel on business, and to satisfy this demand the shipping lines began another round of construction. Many of this new generation of cruise liners were built in the United States, where the shipyards had suffered no war damage. Henceforth, there were only two classes of travel, on the whole, and luxury now gave way to practicality. The number of inside cabins was reduced, air conditioning became standard, and gradually all new vessels were fitted with antiroll stabilizers.

43 | The arrivals and departures of the great ocean liners have always been a favorite subject for artists. This painting by Charles Pears depicts the *Queen Mary* docking at Southampton with the aid of two tugboats on March 27, 1936. A group of fitters from John Brown of Clydebank are watching from the dock in their work clothes as they prepare to put the finishing touches on the ship when she arrives.

44–45 | Cut-away diagram of the SS *France*. Bought by Norwegian Caribbean Lines in 1974 and rechristened first the *Norway* and subsequently *Blue Lady*, she was broken up at the Alang yards in India in 2008.

43

44

Pierre PARRETON
MicheLezla 61

45

46 | The spectacle of the Palazzo Ducale and Piazza San Marco in Venice is even more sublime for those fortunate enough to view it from the deck of an ocean liner. Here, passengers line the handrails of the MSC liner *Poesia* to enjoy the magnificent spectacle.

47 | A design by the French architect Jean-Philippe Zoppini for the world's largest floating structure, heavily inspired by Jules Verne's *Propeller Island*. With the rapid growth in cruises, Zoppini's AZ Island might yet become a reality.

The golden age of ocean liners drew to a close in 1957, the year in which for the first time passengers traveling by air outnumbered those traveling by sea. From 1954, Boeing B-707s were flying from Paris to New York in six hours, and soon every airline had a fleet of long-haul and medium-haul jets. But old habits died hard, and there was still time for the French Line to launch the *France* in 1961 and Cunard to launch the *Queen Elizabeth 2,* popularly known as the *QE2*, in 1969.

Unable to compete with air travel for speed, the shipping lines now concentrated on the well-established field of cruises. From 1962, the *France* alternated a regular scheduled service with cruises to the Caribbean. Her two world tours, in 1972 and 1974, were undisputed successes, and it soon became clear that cruises were destined for major expansion. While they awaited the delivery of the latest generation of liners, specially designed for this new area of activity, the shipping lines busily adapted their newest ships to make them suitable. Now, in the early years of the twenty-first century, the world's seas are crisscrossed by superliners even more colossal than their predecessors. Jules Verne's *Propeller Island* may just be about to cross the line from fantasy to reality.

THE MEDITERRANEAN
AND THE SUEZ CANAL

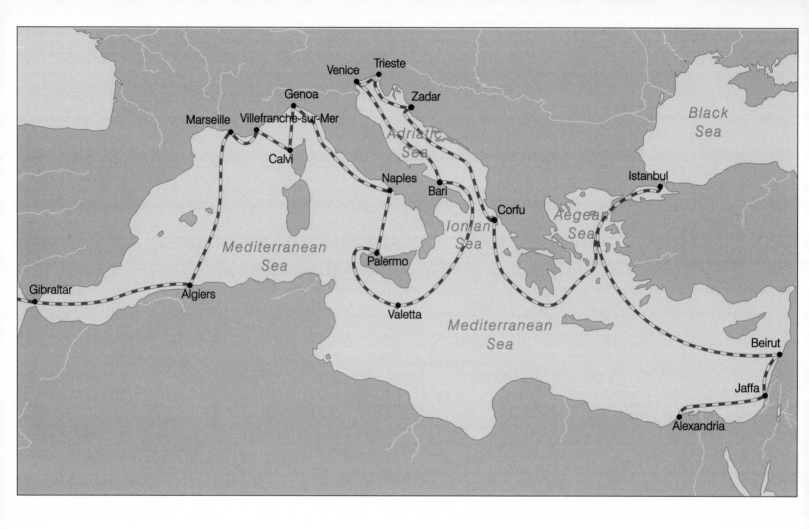

48 | Passengers boarding a steamer at Algiers, c.1900.

51 | Poster advertising the Compagnie Générale Transatlantique. For many years France enjoyed a monopoly over these routes, which were officially included in the same category as its coastal services.

On November 17, 1869, the French imperial yacht *Aigle* with Empress Eugénie on board officially opened the Suez Canal. Ferdinand de Lesseps, president of the Suez Canal Company, and members of the company's administrative council, had boarded ship at Port Said in Egypt. Published in 1876, Percy Fitzgerald's book, *The Great Canal at Suez*, gives an account of the opening of the canal and the festivities surrounding the momentous occasion:

> The illumination and display of fireworks at Port Said that evening were magnificent. Each of the streets had been adorned with a double line of red flagstaffs with the crescent, different colored banners, and lines of colored lanterns. Many of the houses had hung out flags. As evening fell, and the sun sank behind the long straight line of sand, the view from the ships was very picturesque. The deep glow faded from the sky, and the forest of masts now denuded of their colors, became confused and indistinct, faint lines of light seemed to creep like golden gossamer threads across the sky. Long lines of lanterns, festooned from mast to mast and down the lines of rigging, everywhere made their appearance. Some of the men-of-war could be traced by the lights placed at every porthole. Nor was the scene less brilliant on shore. There the long lines of lanterns marked out the streets; while away far to the right the Arab town and the tents of the troops were

51

marked out by the long lines of light. The piers and breakwater were lighted up by tar barrels placed at short intervals. Over all the moon shone brightly, while the flashing electric light upon the summit of the lofty lighthouse at one moment flashed out intensely bright, and then faded into comparative darkness. In the background, behind the Royal yachts, flights of rockets continued to ascend, lighting up the scene, now with colored stars, now with showers of falling gold.

After nearly eleven years of excavation and endless technical, political, and financial problems, the link between East and West was finally complete. With the opening of the Suez Canal, the Mediterranean became the fastest, most economical, and safest route between the Atlantic and Indian oceans. Just 120 miles (193 kilometers) long and 623 feet (190 meters) wide, the canal meant that

ships no longer had to round Africa via the Cape of Good Hope: for European shipping lines it was revolutionary. European operators were best placed to take full advantage of the new opportunities presented by the canal, and all the more so as the new market for cultural tourism was beginning. A mere decade after the canal opened to shipping, passenger traffic had increased considerably. To respond to this demand, the Compagnie Paquet brought a number of new steam packets into

52 Left | Steamers off Jaffa, c.1910. Pilgrims and tourists wishing to visit the Holy Places flocked to Palestine long before the creation of the state of Israel. The absence of a harbor and the presence of offshore reefs conspired to make disembarkation challenging. A flotilla of small boats would ferry passengers ashore, crossing a sand bar with a perilous reputation. On April 27, 1905, in her book *Croisière en Méditerranée* Mme Hériot noted: "As we reached the line of white water, we could not suppress a flutter of alarm. The boat reared up and was carried round in something resembling a whirlpool; then following a turn of breathtaking skill, we made landfall on the quay."

operation on services between Marseille, Syria, and the Black Sea. Not to be left behind, Messageries Maritimes offered services throughout the Indian Ocean, the Far East, the Black Sea, and the Middle East. In the end, only competition from Italian lines prevented France from imposing a complete monopoly on the Mediterranean. In 1931, weary of the unequal struggle, the Italian lines decided to come together to present a united front in the form of the powerful Italia Flotta Riunite.

But the French lines were determined not to give an inch to the Italian opposition, and their tenacity paid off: in 1889, they obtained the exclusive rights to routes between France, Algeria, and Tunisia. North Africa was in fact remarkably well served, largely thanks to mail contracts concluded with the French government. Just before World War I, Algeria received an average of two postal services daily. The Compagnie Générale Transatlantique operated these routes jointly with the Compagnie de Navigation Mixte, which put its remarkable *Gouverneur*-type liners into service, followed by the *El-Goléa* and her equally successful successors.

Passengers crossing the Mediterranean at this time fell into several categories. First came business travelers with

trading interests in Turkey, the Levant, or North Africa. Then came colonial administrators and army officers on the way out to their postings, some of whom extended their journey beyond Suez to the Indies and Far East. And last, but of growing importance, came the tourists. Since the return of Napoleon and the scholars who accompanied him on his Egyptian campaign, Europe had been fascinated by Egyptian civilization. For every person of culture—or with aspirations in that direction—a visit to Egypt was mandatory. Scholars, artists, and writers flocked there, along with an entire social class hungry for intellectual improvement. The wealthiest among these boasted their own yachts. Others traveled to Alexandria before chartering a felucca to carry them up the Nile to Cairo and the adjoining archaeological sites. The year 1869 saw the advent of cruises up the Nile, when the Englishman Thomas Cook organized his first Nile Tour. It was to prove the point of departure for an activity of ever-burgeoning popularity. For while Egypt remained the most favored destination for tourists, every country along the Mediterranean coast was also bursting with archaeological treasures.

A visit to Italy was compulsory for every artist, but in the early twentieth century the roads were dreadful and the

railways barely tolerable. In these conditions, steamers were still the best means of getting from one city to another, departing from Marseille and stopping at Genoa, Pisa, Rome, Naples, Bari, and Ancona. At Venice passengers disembarked, to continue their journey—after visiting *La Serenissima*—aboard the Orient Express. The shipping lines did well out of this arrangement, as cruises ensured a steady income.

Henceforth, a traveler from Europe could reach India without disembarking, and the shipping lines built new

liners specially designed for long voyages: larger and faster vessels on which passengers would spend not just a few days, but several weeks. Architects improved the level of comfort and increased the number of outside cabins, achieving this by placing the dining rooms in the interior of the vessel, beneath the main deck. Rising through several decks, these lofty chambers successfully provided the requisite space for rows of cabins.

Taking their inspiration from developments in liners on the North Atlantic route, architects now cut out sections of the promenade deck in order to insert large glazed domes through which light could penetrate the spaces below. The great canteens of the heroic age of steam travel vanished, and passengers in first and second class now took their meals at smaller tables seating six or eight. Third class, meanwhile, gradually disappeared altogether. In fine weather, passengers could indulge in the delicious pastime of leaning on the ship's rail and observing passing ships, the Mediterranean being too confined a space for liners to be without company for long. Until World War I, many would still be under sail, and watching their graceful movements proved a source of endless fascination and delight.

Passenger liners would also encounter warships of every size and nationality. But the most common form of shipping was naturally the merchant steamer, and passengers would vie with each other to spot which line these vessels belonged to according to their funnels. The funnels of the Compagnie Générale Transatlantique were red with a white band, as were those of the Cunarders, though these also sported a shield with a golden lion holding the globe between its paws. P&O funnels were yellow, and those of the Italian Line white with an unequal vertical tricolor of green, white, and red. Sometimes the

56 | The port of Palermo, c.1910. Italy at this time was the tourist destination *par excellence*, with Sicily forming its natural extension.

57 | The music room on board the Messageries Maritimes mail steamer *Champollion*, showing the Egyptian-inspired decorative theme favored throughout the vessel's public rooms. Launched at La Ciotat in March 1924, the *Champollion* sailed to Syrian ports via Alexandria and Port Said.

symbols chosen gave rise to amusement. The Chargeurs Réunis embellished the white band on their yellow funnels with a row of five red stars intended to represent the five continents, though sailors were not slow to dub the company the Cognac Line or Brandy Line. The emblems and colors of the various lines' funnels formed a veritable heraldry of the high seas, and still today they remain the signatures of the world's shipping lines.

The years between the wars, glittering on land, were equally splendid at sea. Art Nouveau made a magnificent entrance in the decoration of both public and private rooms. In fact the new aesthetic was also imposed by necessity, as in the wake of a number of catastrophic fires at sea, new safety regulations prohibited the use of large wooden panels and other combustible materials. In their place, architects turned to glass, metal, marble, and lacquer, while designers created new styles, often inspired by the liners' regular ports of call. Italy was evoked by a plethora of paintings, statues, and furniture recalling the Roman empire; Greece by classical statuary, or rather copies of it; and Egypt by the reproductions of ancient Egyptian art that graced the majority of liners passing through the Suez Canal.

Up until the end of the 1960s, when air travel definitively usurped sea travel as the most popular method of transporting passengers, cruises were concentrated in the Mediterranean. In addition to Egypt and Italy, passengers visited Greece, Turkey, and the countries of North Africa. Still today, the cultural aspect of Mediterranean cruises continues to attract many tourists. But this new generation of tourists tends to be younger, and more interested in the activities pursued by their distant predecessors than in sunbathing on deck. Cruises have become a more democratic pursuit. In response to the requirements of this new clientele, the shipping lines now lay greater emphasis on convivial entertainment and activities both on board and on land. Never have there been so many cruise ships plying the Mediterranean, ushering in a new golden age of travel, in which the goal is not to go faster, but to ensure that travelers return home with a host of happy memories.

He saw it once more, that landing-place that takes the breath away, that amazing group of incredible structures the Republic set up to meet the awe-struck eye of the approaching seafarer: the airy splendor of the palace and the Bridge of Sighs, the columns of lion and saint on the shore, the glory of the projecting flank of the fairy temple, the vista of gateway and clock. Looking, he thought that to come to Venice by the station is like entering a palace by the back door. No one should approach, save by the high seas as he was doing now, this most improbable of cities.

THOMAS MANN, *Death in Venice,* 1912

We are on board the steamer *Rameses,* the largest and best of Cook's steamers on the Nile. She carries sixty-two passengers, and all her berths are full. There are about forty ladies and twenty men, most of whom are English and Americans; some are traveling for health, some for pleasure. Among the latter are a few sketchers, ever content, for the light and shade of Egypt always give them something new; among the former are a few grumblers, who grumble even in Egypt, and therefore would grumble anywhere.

Close to the landing-stage are the crowds of Nile boats—the dahabeahs of the people and the dahabeahs of the rich, all alike in shape and rig, but differing greatly in either being decked and fitted up—something in the style of a fashionable house-boat, or in being untidy, dirty, and picturesque. Most of them have Arabs on board: some are doing nothing; some, half-nude, are mending their clothes; some are talking; some sleeping; but most are lazily watching the great steamer get ready for its start.

After a little delay we are off, away from the great fleet of boats, with their graceful long masts and beams. We steam past Cairo, with a beautiful last view of the citadel, which seems to glide along with us for a short distance, with its mountains behind and palm trees in front.

HELEN MARY TIRARD, *Sketches from a Nile Steamer,* January 31, 1891

There is no more delightful trip by steamer than that which starts from Trieste, say, in one of the new beautiful boats of the Austrian-Lloyd, the *Carinthia;* halting at Corfu, threading the channel of the Ionian Islands, hugging the coast-line of Greece, unique in the glory of polychromatic haze that envelops its barrenness in a radiance of transparencies, rounding the Peloponnesus, and giving you the first glimpses of the Plain of Attica as you approach the harbor of Piraeus—what a banquet of classical reminiscences! There before you in the background are the large curves of famed Pente-licus with the white seams of its marble quarries, the lofty cone of lonely Lycabettus, and the nearer lower levels of the Acropolis rock with its darkling outlines of the Parthenon. It is only some thirty-five hours from the Piraeus to Constantinople, but what a vista of memories revives and gathers round each spot you pass in crossing the upper waters of the Aegean!

JOHN PATRICK BARRY, *At the Gates of the East,* 1906

65 | A crocodile album of a Hapag Mediterranean cruise, c.1910, a sumptuous keepsake presented to the wealthy passengers in first class.

66 | Passengers on the *Empress of India* of Canadian Pacific Lines on a Mediterranean cruise in 1930 disembark at Gibraltar where carriages line up to take them into town.

67 | A lithograph by Charles Pears for the Empire Marketing Board, c.1928, shows *Britannia* ruling the waves. It is no coincidence that a battleship of the Mediterranean Squadron is seen patrolling in the background–under the confident gaze of an upper-class British family bound for an outpost of the empire.

68 Left | Passengers on the deck of RMS *Atlantis* in the 1930s. Formerly a Pacific Steam Navigation Company steamer plying routes to South America, in 1929 the *Atlantis* was converted into a cruise liner with accommodation for 450 first-class passengers.

68 Right | Advertisement for Mediterranean study cruises to the Canaries and Madeira or Greece and the Greek islands in 1907, organized by the *Revue générale des Sciences* aboard the cargo and passenger ship *Ile de France* of the Société Générale de Transport Maritime (SGTM).

69 | The cargo and passenger ship *Ile de France* in dock at Seville in Spain. Following her purchase by the SGTM from a Dutch shipping line in 1900, she was never again to leave Mediterranean waters.

70–71 | The port of Algiers. Passengers arriving here for the first time were surprised to discover a city very reminiscent of the towns of southern France. The seafront architecture, in particular, bears striking similarities to that of Nice or Marseille.

72 | The Hapag steamer *Prinzessin Victoria Luise* in harbor at Algiers. This elegant liner was built in 1900–01 at the Blohm & Voss shipyards in Hamburg. Generally credited as the first vessel to be purpose-built as a cruise ship, she sailed principally between Germany and the Caribbean, making an occasional appearance, as here, in the Mediterranean. She ran aground and sank off Jamaica in 1907.

73 | The Hamburg Amerika Linie steamer *Normannia* in harbor at Algiers,

c.1900. Passengers are being ferried back to the vessel by local boats, as the ship's own boats are still in position. The *Normannia* could accommodate 420 passengers in first class, 172 in second class, and 700 in third. From the outset she sailed the New York route, with the addition of regular forays into the Mediterranean to pick up emigrants to the United States. Bought in 1899 by the Compagnie Générale Transatlantique, she was renamed *Aquitaine* and sailed the Le Havre–New York route.

74 | The port of La Joliette, near Marseille, was always bustling with activity, with piles of merchandise of all kinds waiting on its quays. The Compagnie des Messageries Maritimes had its offices and loading piers here.

75 Left | A stylish couple enjoys a stroll on the deck of a steamer, c. 1920.

75 Right | In the 1930s, the Société Maritime Nationale, which ran the mail service between the French mainland and Corsica, offered cruises from Corsica to Malta via Tunisia.

76 | Around 1905, a trio of well-dressed ladies strikes an elegant pose on the harbor front at Villefranche-sur-Mer near

Nice. On the horizon, the Hapag steamer *Prinzessin Victoria Luise* may be seen emerging from a soft mist.

77 | Page from a photograph album of a Mediterranean cruise on board the RMS *Atlantis* in the 1920s.

78–79 | Tucked between the mountains and the sea, and with poor communications with its hinterland, Genoa very early developed a busy life as a commercial port. In the 1920s, the Italian government supported its development by sponsoring the creation of scheduled steamer services. By 1925 there were already over 100 of these, including new routes that enabled Italian shipping lines to extend their presence into waters where hitherto they had been a rare sight, such as Genoa–Bombay and Genoa–Dakar–Matadi–Loboto. This photograph, taken in the late 1800s, shows that sailing ships were still common at this time, and that the majority of steamers retained their sailing rig as an alternative form of propulsion.

80 | This yacht-like vessel in harbor at Naples is in fact a typical cargo and passenger ship of the early twentieth century.

81 | The port at Naples—the great rival to Genoa and Trieste—had seen the launch on September 27, 1818 of the first steamship in Mediterranean waters, the *Real Ferdinando I*, bound for America. Following the unification of Italy, the port of Naples slid into a steep decline. Only in the early twentieth century did it experience a revival in its fortunes as it focused on passenger transport, particularly emigration. In 1925, over a million passengers moved through the port of Naples and in the 1930s new docks and infrastructure were built to support increased passenger volume. In 2007 nearly 9 million passengers moved through the port.

82–83 | The port of Naples in the early twentieth century. Mme Heriot described arriving here on a small cruise steamer in 1905: Hardly had the ship docked before the passengers were "surrounded, besieged, assailed by swarms of beggars and pedlars." But this was nothing compared with the stench that choked their nostrils and throats: "Our lungs were filled with this stench, which emanated from all the neighboring tanneries. Mercifully, the health officer proposed to attest in

63

writing to the health-giving properties of this appalling odor. And so we were reassured." The next morning, mercifully, the passengers were taken by carriage to spend the day in Pompeii.

84 | Gondolas moored at dawn off Piazza San Marco in Venice, awaiting the arrival of La Serenissima's crowds of tourists, many of whom will have disembarked from visiting cruise liners.

85 | The Hapag liner *Meteor* steams past the Doges' Palace, c.1910. In the foreground is a lateen-rigged tartan, the traditional Mediterranean cargo vessel.

86 | Passengers from a small steamer docked at Trieste gather at the foot of the gangplanks, awaiting the signal from the crew to board the ship again.

87 | The jetty at Abbazia in Istria. From the mid-nineteenth century Abbazia (now Opatija in Croatia) was a highly fashionable seaside resort, favored by crowned heads, aristocrats, wealthy tourists and famous artistes. The celebrated dancer Isadora Duncan (1877–1927) loved it here, finding inspiration in the trembling of the palm leaves in the morning breeze.

88 | Photochrom image of a small steam cruiser taking on passengers at the Croatian port of Zadar, opposite Ancona, in the late nineteenth century.

89 | The palace that Sissi, Empress of Austria, built in 1891 in a small mountain village some 6 miles (10 kilometers) from Corfu, which she called the Achilleion, became—after her assassination seven years later—a place of pilgrimage. This photograph, taken in 1910, shows a handful of local people, some in national dress, taking the air beside the harbor. Mme Hériot wrote of Corfu: "At around ten o'clock in the morning, the coast of Corfu appeared . . . unfolding before our eyes, which they refreshed with their greenery. At midday we entered the harbor, mooring close to the citadel. . . . All was silence; the quays deserted; the town slumbering. But the sun beat down on us . . . Sheltering beneath our awnings or taking refuge in our cabins, we waited to disembark, to be able to breathe."

90–91 | "We came here through the Dardanelles, arriving in the morning sunshine. No pen can well depict the glory of the view, for on the earth's broad face I know no fairer scene than

this. Venice rising from the sea; Naples's amphitheatre of palaces reflected in her gorgeous bay; Genoa or Buenos Ayres—all are beauteous gems, but all fade before this vision fair of paradise. The curious old battlemented walls, the confused terraced roofs, the palaces in marble rows along the waterfront, towers, gilded tips of lofty minarets, and noble mosques with clustered domes, the cypress groves and arsenals, and over all the soft blue sky—there is no sight so fair in all the world beside."
D.N. Richardson, *A Girdle Round the Earth*, 1888.

92 | "The port of Beirut is very rocky; ships are obliged to drop anchor in the harbor that I saw before me; and even this is very bad," noted Count Charles de Pardieu in 1851. "The cargo is unloaded onto boats which themselves are unable to reach the quayside, so that the Arabs are forced to plunge into the water in order to carry out the unloading. The quay, which lay beneath my window, is fairly narrow and continually battered by the sea, with waves breaking over it."
This photograph shows the harbor around 1880.

93 | Beirut was one of the pearls of the Mediterranean, where tourists loved to wander through the bazaar and the bustling, vaulted streets, with their perpetual contrasts of warm shadows and pools of dazzling light.

94 | The port of Alexandria as it would have looked to passengers arriving in Egypt in the late nineteenth century. By this time a pier had been constructed, so avoiding the necessity of ferrying steamer passengers ashore by boat.

95 | According to travelers, the sea approach to Alexandria had little to recommend it. Only when the steamer was within ten miles of the coast would passengers be able to make out its lowest point. The first sight on the horizon would be the Pharos Lighthouse, followed by Pompey's Pillar, the dome of the Ras el-Teen Palace, the Napoleonic windmills at Mex, and finally terra firma beyond Ramleh. At last they could see Alexandria. Half an hour later an Egyptian pilot would come on board and steer the vessel round the jetty, and passengers would disembark at one of the piers. On this photochrom, one sees in the foreground the channel of Mamoudieh, which connects the port to the Nile with a system of locks.

Hamburg-
Amerika Linie

Mittelmeer-Fahrten

68

CROISIÈRES

DE LA
❦ Revue générale des Sciences ❦

Paquebot-yacht ILE-DE-FRANCE
Navire de la *Société générale de Transports maritimes à vapeur*, spécialement aménagé pour la navigation de plaisance et exclusivement affecté aux croisières de la *Revue générale des Sciences*.

42 CHAMBRES A UN LIT — 71 CHAMBRES A DEUX LITS — 10 CHAMBRES A TROIS LITS
En aucun cas les lits ne sont superposés.

3.487 tonneaux de jauge

115 mètres de longueur

12 mètres 50 de largeur

10 mètres de creux

2.400 chevaux

Lumière électrique

Chauffage par circulation d'eau

Grands Salons

214 places

7 salles de bain

2 chambres noires pour la photographie

Pont-promenade

CROISIÈRE DE PAQUES 1907 ❦ CROISIÈRE DE SEPTEMBRE 1907

Aux Canaries
et à Madère.

Cette croisière fera voir en détail : la GRANDE CANARIE (avec LA LUZ, LAS PALMAS, SAN MATEO); l'île de TÉNÉRIFFE (avec OROTAVA, SANTA-CRUZ DE TÉNÉRIFFE, GUIMAR, les volcans éteints des CANADAS et le pic de TEYDE); l'île de MADÈRE à l'époque la plus favorable pour jouir de sa merveilleuse végétation.

Elle comprendra de nombreuses escales et excursions intermédiaires : à ALMERIA, en Espagne; à LISBONNE, BELEM et CINTRA, en Portugal; à TANGER, MAZAGAN et MOGADOR, au Maroc.

NOTA. — Si, chose peu probable, des événements politiques venaient à s'opposer à des descentes sur la côte atlantique du Maroc, d'autres escales seraient effectuées en compensation.

Le voyage sera dirigé par M. AUGUSTIN BERNARD, professeur à la Sorbonne.

Spécimen des cabines d'*Ile-de-France*.

En Grèce
et aux Iles Grecques

Cette croisière permettra d'étudier tous les grands sanctuaires archéologiques de la Grèce et de ses îles.

Elle fera voir : OLYMPIE, DELPHES CORINTHE, SPARTE, ATHÈNES (pendant cinq jours, avec excursions à DAPHNÉ, ELEUSIS et KEPHISIA), EGINE, NAUPLIE, ARGOS TYRINTHE, MYCÈNES, EPIDAURE; RHAMNONTE, le CAP SUNIUM, VOLO et la *Thessalie* (mont PÉLION, PHARSALE, KALABAKA, les MÉTÉORES, LARISSA, et la vallée de TEMPE); DÉLOS; SANTORIN; la *Crète* (CANDIE, KNOSSOS, LA CANÉE, LA SUDE), la *Messénie* (KALAMATA, MESSÈNE et le mont ITHÔME); en *Sicile*, MESSINE et TAORMINE.

Cette croisière sera dirigée par un historien-archéologue hautement qualifié.

RENSEIGNEMENTS :

Pour recevoir franco les programmes détaillés de chacune des Croisières de la *Revue générale des Sciences* s'adresser à la Direction de la Revue :

22, rue du Général-Foy, à Paris.

69

LE CIRCUIT
AJACCIO
TUNIS
MALTE
TUNIS
BASTIA
EST UN VÉRITABLE CIRCUIT
DE CROISIÈRE

AJACCIO:

SON GOLFE,
LES ÎLES SANGUINAIRES,
LES SOUVENIRS NAPOLÉONIENS.

TUNIS:

LA VILLE MUSULMANE.
SES PALAIS, SES MUSÉES
DE CARTHAGE
ET DU
BARDO

MALTE:

LA "POMME D'OR" DE
LA MÉDITERRANÉE.
LES GLORIEUSES SURVIVANCES
DES CHEVALIERS DE MALTE.

BASTIA:

LA MÉTROPOLE PITTORESQUE
DE LA CORSE
CENTRE D'EXCURSIONS EN MONTAGNE,
AU GOLFE DE SAINT-FLORENT,
AU CAP CORSE.

SOCIÉTÉ MARITIME NATIONALE

CORSE TUNISIE MALTE

76

9791 2399

9791 2400

9791 2402

Cⁱᵉ Gˡᵉ
s/s VILLE D'ALGER
TRANSATLANTIQUE

77

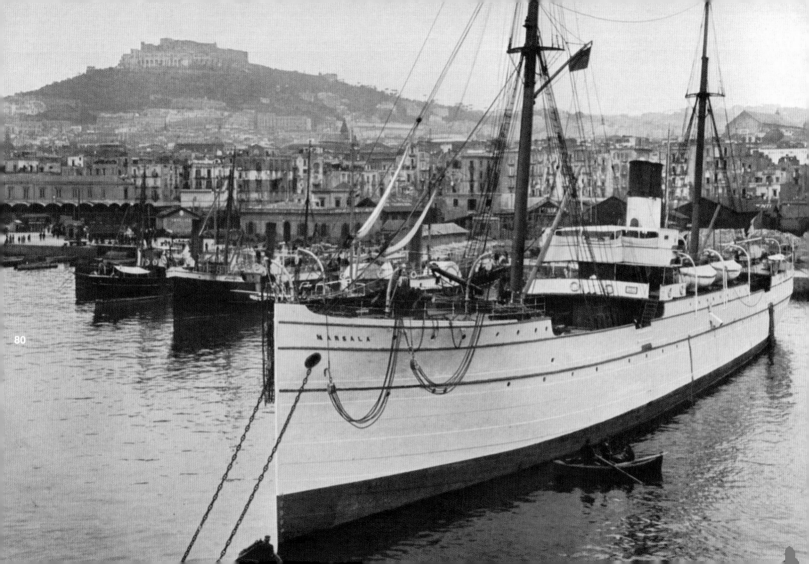

83

89

90

91

94

95

THE TRANSATLANTIC CROSSING AND THE BLUE RIBAND

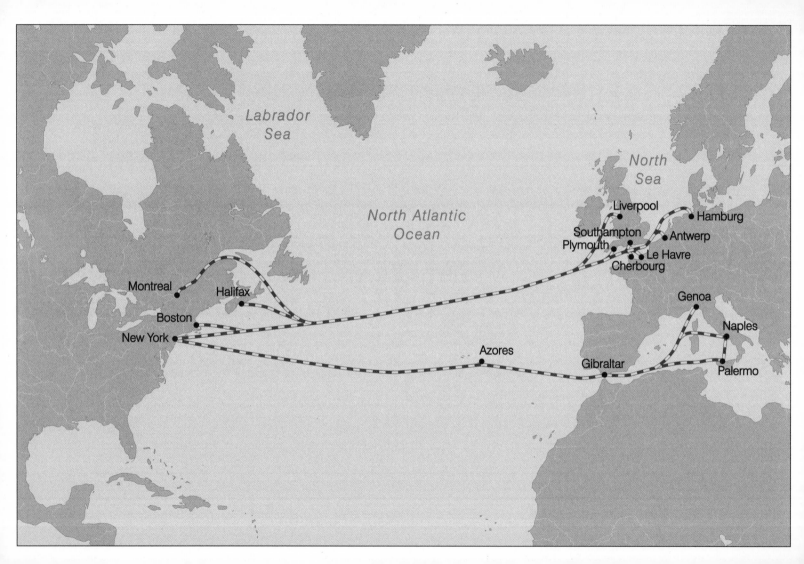

96 | Setting sail on the *Imperator*, c.1914.

99 | The paddle steamer *Brittannia* kept her sailing rig as a supplementary form of power. In 1840, she completed a crossing of the Atlantic in fifteen days and ten hours.

On the evening of April 22, 1838, the SS *Sirius* steamed into New York harbor. The little Irish paddle steamer, operated by the St. George Steam Packet Company and chartered for this voyage by the British and American Steam Navigation Company, had left Cork eighteen days earlier. The crossing had been a difficult one, with heavy seas, hail, and snow, not to mention the atmosphere of extreme tension on board. In the cramped space—she measured only 177 feet (54 meters) in length—driven to his wit's end by the fretting of his seasick passengers and the exasperation of his exhausted crew, the captain had more than once been reduced to brandishing his pistol in order to restore order. This was no ordinary crossing, however, but a resounding achievement: when it finally arrived in New York, the *Sirius* became the first ship to cross the Atlantic exclusively by steam power. On the way she had consumed not merely 500 tons of coal, but also virtually everything else on board that could be burned, including the spare yards and mast for the rigging (with which early steamers were still equipped).

The following day, as New York was preparing to celebrate this remarkable event, came a dramatic coup as the SS *Great Western* of the Great Western Steamship

99

Company, another British vessel and the little steamer's great rival in this epic race, also entered harbor after crossing the Atlantic by steam. Moreover, as she had left Europe four days later, on April 8, she had beaten the *Sirius* hands down. The *Great Western* had completed the crossing in just fifteen and a half days.

This was the start of a competition that thrilled the world for over a century. The North Atlantic crossing was to be the scene of epic struggles between numerous maritime companies and the countries they represented, with ocean liners of herculean proportions unleashed at top speed on one of the most prestigious of the world's ocean routes— and one of the most dangerous. But what lay at stake, a heady cocktail of national pride and commercial profit, was equally momentous. Whenever a ship set a new record, a whole country celebrated in jubilation, while the victorious shipping company would see its bookings soar—until another great liner arrived to steal the record. And all set against a background of ever more colossal investments and unprecedented risks, in a competitive frenzy that in the end was simply to run out of these epic duelists of the sea.

The magnificent exploit of the *Sirius* and the *Great Western* was the signal for battle to begin. Not until the late nineteenth century did the term Blue Riband widely come to represent the fastest Atlantic crossing of a passenger vessel, and with it the right to fly from its mast a blue pennant of a length proportionate to the average speed in knots maintained during the voyage. However, *Sirius* is universally recognized to be the first record holder, as the ship that started the craze. In 1934, British businessman and parliamentarian Harold K. Hales introduced the North Atlantic Blue Riband Challenger Trophy, known as the Hales Trophy. The four-foot-tall silver trophy weighed nearly a hundred pounds and depicted a winged messenger carrying a ship astride a globe above Poseidon, the Greek god of the seas.

However, no formal trophy was needed; in the nineteenth century competition to make the fastest Atlantic crossing was fierce. Following the *Great Western* came the British and North American Royal Mail Steam-Packet, founded by Samuel Cunard in 1839, which that same year launched its first liner built specifically for the transatlantic crossing, RMS *Britannia*. On July 4, 1840, she left port in Liverpool on her maiden voyage and steamed straight into the record books as the fastest transatlantic liner, earning the first Blue Riband for Cunard, which

101 | The *Baltic* was
built in New York in 1850
by Jacob Bell for the
Collins Line. In addition
to her paddle wheels
she also retained the rig
of a three-masted sailing
ship.

followed this with victories by two other liners, thus holding the record until 1848. Speed was then and for many years to come a shipping line's most powerful selling point, even if passengers sometimes regretted their choice once on board. In his *American Notes*, Charles Dickens gave a memorable account of his January 1842 crossing on the *Britannia*:

> But what the agitation of a steam-vessel is, on a bad winter's night in the wild Atlantic, it is impossible for the most vivid imagination to conceive. To say that she is flung down on her side in the waves, with her masts dipping into them, and that, springing up again, she rolls over on the other side,

until a heavy sea strikes her with the noise of a hundred great guns, and hurls her back—that she stops, and staggers, and shivers, as though stunned, and then, with a violent throbbing at her heart, darts onward like a monster goaded into madness, to be beaten down, and battered, and crushed, and leaped on by the angry sea—that thunder, lightning, hail, and rain, and wind, are all in fierce contention for the mastery—that every plank has its groan, every nail its shriek, and every drop of water in the great ocean its howling voice—is nothing. To say that all is grand, and all appalling and horrible in the last degree, is nothing. Words cannot express it. Thoughts cannot convey it. Only a dream can call it up again, in all its fury, rage, and passion.

His attempts to administer brandy to his terrified wife and her companions were doomed to comic failure:

> It being impossible to stand or sit without holding on, they were all heaped together in one corner of a long sofa— a fixture, extending entirely across the cabin—where they clung to each other in momentary expectation of being drowned.

Although Dickens could be forgiven a degree of hyperbole in his mission to entertain his readers, this crossing was indeed one of the stormiest in years. Nor was the specter of drowning a mere idle fear or vague

LENGTH OF DECK, 291 FEET.
BREADTH OF 20 46 .
DEPTH OF HOLD, 32 .

2 SIDE LEVER ENGINES, 95 IN. DIAMETER.
9 FEET STROKE.
900 NOMINAL HORSE POWER.

U. S. M. Steamship ATLANTIC, *James West, Commander.*

EDWARD K. COLLINS, ESQ. AGENT AND SUPERINTENDENT.

Builder, W. H. Brown. —— Engines, Stillman, Allen & Co. —— Architect and Decorator, Geo. Platt. —— Joiner, Robert Latou. —— Painter, Stephen Squires. —— Upholsterer, James Phyfe.

NEW YORK PUBLISHED BY N. CURRIER

| Equipped with paddle wheels and the rig of a three-masted schooner, the *Atlantic* was the first steamer put into service by the Collins Line.

apprehension: ships were regularly lost on the North Atlantic crossing, and the newspapers offered graphic accounts of these tragedies, with no traumatic detail spared. In these circumstances, the wonder is that passengers continued to board these boats at all, let alone to clamor for ever-faster crossings. Attempts to beat the reigning record all too often came at catastrophic cost.

The short-lived triumphs of the American shipping lines tell their own story. The New-York and Havre Steamship Navigation Company made a fleeting appearance among the laureates in the 1840s, before losing both its liners in rapid succession. In 1849, the Collins Line signed a contract with the US Postmaster General Office for the transport of passengers and post between New York and Liverpool, with fortnightly crossings in the summer and monthly departures in winter. Its liners were not only among the most luxurious yet known, but also the fastest: the *Pacific* carried off the Blue Riband in 1851, to be beaten later that year by another Collins liner, the *Baltic*, which had to cede the honor the following year to a third, the *Arctic*. But these victories were followed by a string of tragedies from which the company was never to recover. In 1854, the *Arctic* was in collision with another ship off the coast of Newfoundland and sank, with the loss of over 300 lives. These included Mrs. Collins, wife of the line's founder, their only daughter, and their youngest son. In 1856 tragedy struck again, when the *Pacific* steamed out of Liverpool and vanished, never to be seen again. In 1858 the Collins Line was declared bankrupt.

Contemporary accounts indicate the acute levels of consternation aroused among the general public by such catastrophes. In his memoir *A Small Boy and Others,* Henry James described an evening at theatre in New York when he was a child. Although it was a lighthearted piece, he recalled that the tremendous tension among the audience owing to the fact that the *Atlantic,* another Collins liner, was several days late in arriving. Everyone feared the worst. When one of the actors came on stage to announce that the liner had docked safely:

> "Ladies and gentlemen, I rejoice to be able to tell you that the good ship *Atlantic* is safe!" the house broke into such plaudits, so huge and prolonged a roar of relief, as I had never heard the like of and which gave me my first measure of a great immediate public emotion . . . It was a moment of the golden age—representing too but a snatch of elation, since the wretched *Arctic* had gone down in mortal woe and her other companion the *Pacific* leaving England a few

months later and under the interested eyes of our family group, then temporarily settled in London, was never heard of more.

Though not in competition for the Blue Riband, Canada made a modest contribution to the transatlantic service from 1854, when the Montreal Ocean Steamship Company, known as the Allan Line, inaugurated a service between Quebec and Liverpool. Although the Allan Line vessels could not compete in luxury with the great liners, they offered an alternative summer route passing to the north of the island of Newfoundland, so shortening the voyage by a third in comparison with the crossing from New York to Le Havre or Liverpool. The route was not without its perils, however: while pack ice, icebergs, and ice floes offered magnificent spectacles for the passengers on board, they also posed a real danger of collision—a risk amplified by the fogs that might suddenly descend in these waters. Once these dangers had been negotiated, the vessels then steamed up the great Gulf of St Lawrence, one of the most magnificent approaches to the New World.

In the 1850s, new and infinitely more formidable contenders emerged, as Hamburg-Amerika (HAPAG) and Norddeutscher Lloyd (NDL) began regular services between Hamburg, Bremen, and New York, putting in at Southampton. And finally France made its appearance, represented by the Compagnie Générale Transatlantique, known as the French Line. On

June 28, 1864 the French Line liner *Washington* docked in New York, so inaugurating the company's crossing from Le Havre. In the race for speed, France had a lot of catching up to do. The *Washington* had taken thirteen and a half days: an honorable speed but hardly a record-breaking one, at a time when the Cunarder *Scotia* was already making the crossing in just nine days. But now Cunard found itself

under threat from other British lines: Guion, founded in 1866; Inman, which stole the Blue Riband in 1869 with its *City of Brussels*; and finally the famous and historic White Star Line, which began transatlantic crossings in 1871.

All the outstanding lines in the history of the Blue Riband (with the exception of the Italian lines, who became major players much later) were now in place. With so many different countries now competing, tighter rules had to be drawn up. At this period the point of arrival in New York was accepted as the Sandy Hook Lighthouse, at the entrance to New York harbor. The point of departure had to be taken case by case according to the line, and was

naturally factored into the length and speed of crossing. For German lines, the point of departure was taken as either the Needles, off the western extremity of the Isle of Wight, or the Scilly Isles, depending on whether they put in at Southampton or Plymouth; for CGT liners it was the lighthouse at La Hève; for British liners departing from Liverpool and putting in at the Irish port of Queenstown (today's Cobh), the race started at the Fastnet Rock Lighthouse off the coast of Cork.

The rules for calculating speed and distance were fixed. But what about safety? Two more tragedies were to arouse public concern on this score. In November 1873, the CGT iron steamship *Ville du Havre* collided in mid-Atlantic with the iron clipper *Loch Earn*. The French vessel sank in twelve minutes, with the loss of over 200 lives. Earlier that same year, the White Star steamer *Atlantic* had struck submerged rocks and sank with nearly a thousand passengers and crew on board, half of whom perished. Such catastrophic loss of life had international repercussions, and measures for avoiding unnecessary dangers were suggested. The first of these—which was taken up by several shipping lines—was that ships' captains should be obliged to follow the safest routes.

106 | On November 22, 1873 the iron steamship *Ville du Havre*, crossing the Atlantic with 313 passengers on board, collided with the iron clipper *Loch Earn* and sank, with the loss of 226 lives.

107 | A lifeboat drill on board the Norddeutscher Lloyd steamer *Kaiser Wilhelm II*. Following the sinking of the *Titanic*, safety exercises such as this were a serious matter for both crew and passengers.

108

108 | The smoking room on the *Kaiser Wilhelm der Grosse* of the Norddeutscher Lloyd line.

109 Right | The *Kaiser Wilhelm der Grosse*. In 1898 this German liner snatched the Blue Riband from the British in a surprise victory.

109 Above | A Norddeutscher Lloyd poster from the 1860s, advertising the sailing of the *Bremen*, the first liner of that name, which retained a three-masted sailing rig.

110 & 111 | The first-class dining room (left) and reading room (right) on the *Kaiser Wilhelm der Grosse*.

110

So carried away were they by the excitement of the race that often they took ill-considered risks, sailing too close inshore when rounding headlands, for example, in order to shave off precious minutes. Other safety measures included taking frequent soundings in foggy conditions, and marking coastal and submerged rocks and reefs with illuminated beacons and buoys.

In a bid to regain public confidence, the French Line launched a propaganda war to publicize all the safety improvements it had introduced on its liners: taking carrier pigeons on board in order to stay in contact with the mainland, fitting vessels with navigation lights visible at long distance, and replacing the statutory white light with a projector with a range of ten nautical miles. When the liner *Amérique* entered Plymouth harbor in March 1876, her splendid external electric lighting caused a sensation. All this notwithstanding, one of the chief aims of the French Line in subsequent years was still to win the coveted Blue Riband. Speeds had to be notched up a gear, come what may. And at last, in 1888, the liner *La Bretagne* carried off the prize for France. Ten years later, in July 1898, the French Line lost her sister ship, *La Bourgogne*, a magnificent vessel capable of carrying 1,500 passengers. Steaming at speed through thick summer fog off Newfoundland, she collided with a smaller boat, the *Cromartyshire*, which holed her. Over 500 people, nearly all passengers, lost their lives. Yet again, the international press was furious in its criticism: what were these gigantic liners doing sailing so close to the coastal waters of Newfoundland, which were crowded for six months of the year by flotillas of sailing boats fishing for cod? What gave experienced ships' captains the right to plough full steam ahead through thick fog in their prodigious vessels, so putting in peril the hundreds of lives entrusted to their care?

The German lines kept a safe distance from these controversies, joining the race only at the turn century, when the scale of their ambition took the public's breath away. The formidable *Kaiser Wilhelm der Grosse* of the Nordeutscher Line, for instance, was a colossus, nearly 656 feet (200 meters) long and capable of carrying nearly 2,000 passengers and crew. This was a superliner, with grandiose lines and breathtaking décor, greeted with unanimous acclaim on her maiden voyage in 1897. Within six months she had set records on both the eastbound and westbound crossings. For a long time, her four funnels (she was the first of the four-funneled liners) were viewed by travelers as

113 | In June 1923, the *Leviathan* of the United States Line—formerly the Hapag liner *Vaterland*, captured during the war—completed its first trials with passengers on board.

113

114 | The Italian liner *Rex*, operated by the Navigazione Generale Italiana and shown here in New York in 1940, was one of the most beautiful pre-war steamers.

115 | Marconi radio operator on board the *Deutschland* of the Hamburg Amerika Linie. The radio was an important piece of equipment for both safety and commercial reasons.

the ultimate safety symbol—to the point where the directors of the White Star Line were to give the *Titanic* four funnels, even though only three of them were working, and the fourth was purely for show. It was a ploy aimed principally at reassuring the immigrants who, at this period, would choose the liner they wanted to travel on from models displayed in travel agents' offices. Sadly, when the *Titanic* sank on April 14, 1912, it took more than 1,500 lives.

The tragedy of the *Titanic* did at least have one positive outcome: the International Conference on the Safety of Life at Sea, which took place in London in January 1914. Sixteen nations took part to decide the measures and exercises to which passengers and crew should in future be subject. And what of the reckless rivalry of the Blue Riband? It was to continue unabated, and in as foolhardy a fashion as ever. Evidence of this came in the form of the triumphant crossing of a newcomer in the field: the Italian liner *Rex*, the pride of Italy and one of the most ostentatiously opulent symbols of Mussolini's vaulting ambitions. Now once again, victory had to be won at all costs, and it was Captain Tarabotto's job to deliver it. The liner left Genoa on August 10, 1933, and from that moment, it is said, Tarabotto stayed constantly on the bridge, scrutinizing the sky and

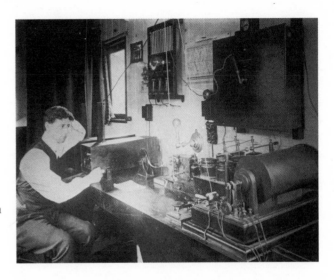

the horizon. Once past Gibraltar the vessel picked up speed, consuming 5 tons (4,600 kg) of fuel every hour. By August 12, the *Rex* had set an impressive average speed of 28.55 knots, more or less matching the speed of the then-record-holder, the German liner *Bremen*. At dawn on the 13th the weather broke. On the 14th, the vessel was still keeping up speed, despite the stormy conditions. By the following morning the wind had dropped, but the *Rex* was now steaming through fog so impenetrable that the most elementary concern for safety would have required it to slow down—and renounce the trophy. Faced with this pea-souper, Tarabotto is reputed to have gone very quiet for a long time, weighing up the pros and cons before giving the order: "*Avanti a tutta forza!*" (full steam ahead). Foghorns blaring, the monster ploughed on at top speed, while the radio operator repeated over and over again a warning to any other ships in the vicinity: "Attention—Direction Ambrose —Approaching at 30 knots." The *Rex* set a new record that she was to keep until 1935, when the *Normandie* wrested it from her.

But the competition had reached the end of its life. The golden age of the transatlantic liner was over. There followed a handful of stately exchanges, as from 1935 the *Queen Mary* (now operated jointly by Cunard and White Star) and the French Line's *Normandie* gracefully passed the Blue Riband to and fro between them, until in 1938 the *Queen Mary* emerged victorious, to keep it for the following fourteen years. Then, on July 3, 1952, the American liner *United States* set the definitive record, never since beaten, of three days, ten hours, and forty minutes for the New York-Le Havre-Southampton crossing.

I have always extended to her more affection than I have to any other ship. I loved her for her gaiety, for her color, for the familiarity with all the world that was in her passenger list. She leaned to excesses in her *décor*; there was something of the fatal woman. She took a *seigneur's* abusive privilege of frowning on the lesser, fatter, longer, more solid boats. Like all aristocrats, she had abominable moods. I think she was more female than all other ships I have known. I think that's why I loved her so.

LUDWIG BEMELMANS,
about the *Normandie*, c. 1946

. . . we drove down to the steamer past the enormous excavations where myriads of men were working and which were to become Grand Central Terminal. It was quite biblical.

Nellie [Eleanor Jacot] had sent flowers, books, magazines and fruit to the steamer for the voyage. I had Flaubert's letters, and Harriet [Levy] had a copy of *Lord Jim* that she considered a tactless choice by the friend who had sent it.

On board was a distinguished oldish man, a commodore, who got into conversation with me when I was reading on the deck after lunch. We spent the greater part of the voyage together. Harriet did not speak to me of the episode but I could see that she considered that I lacked discretion. The commodore and I said a calm good-bye before we got into the launches that were taking us into the harbor of Cherbourg.

We were indeed in France. It was a fête day and there was dancing in the open air. We decided not to take the crowded boat train in the heat of the day but to stay the night in Cherbourg and take a morning train to Paris. Under the hotel window French voices were signing French songs in the mild French air.

ALICE B. TOKLAS, *What is Remembered*, 1963

117

How often have you crossed the ocean. How many people have you met in the crossing, toward how many have you incurred the obligation of rejoining them and how very many are you willing to moisten rapid repetition with angular vibration.

GERTRUDE STEIN, *Saints and Singing*, 1922

When I was first engaged, some fifteen years ago, to start this work . . . I said to the directors of the company that employed me: "Why don't you make a ship look like a ship?" . . . But the answer I was given was that the people who use these ships are not pirates, they do not dance hornpipes; they are mostly seasick American ladies, and the one thing they want to forget when they are on the vessel is that they are on a ship at all. Most of them have got to travel and they object to it very much. In order to impress that point upon me, the Company sent me across the Atlantic. The first day out I enjoyed the beautiful sea, but when we got well onto the Atlantic, there was one thing I craved for as never before, and that was a warm fire and a pink shade. The people who travel on these large ships are the people who live in hotels; they are not ships for sailors or yachtsmen or people who enjoy the sea. They are inhabited by all sorts of people, some of whom are very delicate and stay in their cabin during the whole voyage; others, less delicate, stay in the smoking room all through the voyage. . . . I suggest to you that the transatlantic liner is not merely a ship, she is a floating town with 3,000 passengers of all kinds, with all sorts of tastes, and those who enjoy being there are distinctly in the minority. If we could get ships to look inside like ships, and get people to enjoy the sea, it would be a very good thing; but all we can do, as things are, is to give them gigantic floating hotels.

ARTHUR DAVIS, architect of the *Aquitania,* 1922

The steamer—which, with its machinery on deck, looked, as it worked its long slim legs, like some enormously magnified insect or antediluvian monster—dashed at great speed up a beautiful bay; and presently they saw some heights, and islands, and a long, flat, straggling city.

"And this," said Mr Tapley, looking far ahead, "is the Land of Liberty, is it? Very well. I'm agreeable. Any land will do for me, after so much water!"

CHARLES DICKENS, *The Life and Adventures of Martin Chuzzlewit*, June 1843

121 | Liverpool was the port of registry of large numbers of merchant ships, and the main British shipping lines all had their offices there. But in the early twentieth century this important port for the Atlantic crossing found its position gradually usurped by Southampton, which offered greater potential for growth.

122–23 | The Compagnie Générale Transatlantique steamer *La Bourgogne* at her mooring in the port of Le Havre, before her refurbishment in 1897. On July 4, 1898 this magnificent vessel collided with the large sailing ship *Cromartyshire*. An hour later she sank with the loss of over 500 lives, in the worst disaster ever to befall this shipping line in peacetime.

124 Left | These opera singers boarded ship for Europe in 1908.

124 Right | Menu for a "Welcome Dinner" on board the Norddeutscher Lloyd steamer *Bremen* in 1934.

125 | Five captains of the Hamburg Amerika Linie, recognizable by their four stripes, pose for a group photograph on board the *Imperator*.

126–27 | A lantern slide showing the departure of a steamer in the 1930s.

128 | First-class passengers on board the Cunard Line's *Lusitania*. The ship was sunk by a German torpedo on May 7, 1915.

129 | When the *Vaterland* steamed out of New York on May 26, 1914 the world was still at peace—but not for long.

130 | The *Kronprinz Wilhelm* cruising at full steam in the mid-Atlantic. The standard of service on German liners before World War I was renowned among passengers.

131 | When the *Vaterland* was in dock in New York in 1914, a handful of invited guests were granted the rare privilege of visiting her. These elegant ladies were able to discover the luxury and sheer scale of this colossal liner.

132 | Winter palm gardens were greatly appreciated by passengers as a means of forgetting that they were at sea. As on all other steamers, this elegant facility on the *Kaiserin Auguste Victoria* was strictly reserved for first-class passengers.

133 | Photochrom view of one of the lounges on a Norddeutscher Lloyd liner. The curve of the ceiling corresponds to that of the deck above, a feature designed to lend the timberwork greater resistance. Only details such as this betray the fact that this interior lies deep within a sea-going vessel.

134 | Detail of a stateroom on the Norddeutscher Lloyd steamer *König Albert*. Here it is the portholes that betray the fact that this opulent bedroom is in fact a ship's cabin.

135 | Theodore Roosevelt in a cabin on the SS *Imperator* in June 1914. At this period there were no American transatlantic shipping lines worthy of the name, and the President evidently preferred the comforts of a German liner to the decidedly more Spartan conditions on board a warship of the US Navy.

136 | These children who have sailed from Europe will shortly disembark in Canada. Their parents, meanwhile, have probably gone to fill out the forms required on arrival.

137 | These immigrants on a transatlantic steamer have come up on the foredeck to get a breath of fresh air. Many of them are bundled in blankets against the cold: a stiff sea breeze was far preferable to the stifling atmosphere in steerage.

138 Left | The music room aboard the SS *Columbus*, put into service in June 1922.

138–39 Center | The music room of the SS *Kronprinz Wilhelm*, c.1900.

139 Right | After World War I, bathrooms became standard in first-class accommodation. This beautiful young woman appears to appreciate her private facilities aboard the *Columbus* of the Norddeutscher Lloyd line.

140–41 | The Cathay Lounge smoking room on board the Canadian Pacific's *Empress of Britain* was decorated by the artist Edmund Dulac. Built in 1930, this was the most sumptuous liner operating on the transatlantic route to Canada. In winter she undertook cruises to Hong Kong, Cuba, Singapore, and South America.

142 | On board the *Normandie*, operated by the Compagnie Générale Transatlantique, the palatial Grand Salon was the hub of fashionable life. Atmospheric lighting was provided by lighted fountains designed by Auguste Labouret; the immense wall panels were painted and gilded on glass by Jean Dupas, and the columns were by Jean Dunand.

143 | Good taste and discretion were the order of the day in the decorations of this bar on the *Normandie*.

144 | On board the *Bremen*, a squadron of stewards ferries supplies of hot coffee to passengers on deck—in first class only, naturally.

145 | An impressive menu for a copious "Farewell Dinner" on board the Norddeutscher Lloyd liner SS *Berlin*, held on Thursday July 31, 1934.

146 | A Cunard White Star line poster for the *Queen Mary*, launched in 1934 and brought into service two years later. This legendary ocean liner was retired in 1967 and converted into a hotel; she is now moored in Long Beach, California.

147 | A delighted young mother and daughter arrive in New York on the SS *Baltic* in 1907.

148–49 | Arrival in New York on June 21, 1911 of RMS *Olympic* of the White Star Line. J. Bruce Ismay, managing director of the company, looked forward to repeating the success of this maiden voyage with the Titanic, still under construction in Belfast.

150 | Ocean liners of the Hamburg-America Line at the dock in Hoboken, New Jersey, c.1915. In the background is the *Vaterland* (later *Leviathan*). Caught in the U.S. when World War I broke out, British dominance of the seas made the return to Germany of the line's ships impossible. The ships remained in Hoboken until the U.S. entered the war and confiscated the 135-vessel fleet.

151 | Hopeful immigrants disembarking at Ellis Island. Leaving the ravages of mass unemployment behind them, they came to America seeking a better life. But settling in the Promised Land, they must face the formidable procedures of American immigration.

123

124

BEGRÜSSUNGS-ESSEN
WELCOME-DINNER

126

134

139

140

141

ABENDS-ESSEN
DINNER

Ein Vorschlag.

Malossol Kaviar auf Eis

Doppelte Kraftbrühe Aremberg

Palmenmark, Colbert Sauce

Gebratenes steirisches Masthuhn
Kopf-Salat, Französische Marinade

Eisbecher Venus

Käse   Kaffee

Suggestion.

Malossol Caviare on Ice

Consommé double Aremberg

Hearts of Palm Sauce Colbert

Roast Styrian Poularde
Lettuce Salad, French Dressing

Coupe Venus

Cheese   Coffee

DINNER

Hors d'Oeuvre

Malossol Caviare on Ice
Tomato Juice Cocktail

——

Soups

Chicken Cream Soup Sévigué
Consommé double Aremberg
Consommé in Cup hot or cold

——

Fish

Boiled Tench Blue, Melted Butter,
Iced Horse-Radish

——

Roast

Larded Tenderloin of Beef Niçoise

Calf's Head Paganini

Roast Styrian Poularde
Lettuce Salad, French Dressing

——

Hearts of Palm, Sauce Colbert

Sweets

Saxonian Pudding Strawberry Sauce
Coupe Venus

——

Cheese

Choice of Cheese
Butter   Pumpernickel   Radishes

Fruit   Fruit in Season   Dessert

——

Coffee   Demi-Tasse · Sanka Demi-Tasse

——

S. S. "BERLIN"
Tuesday, July 31st 1934

145

CUNARD WHITE STAR
TO EUROPE

147

148

151

The South Atlantic and Caribbean

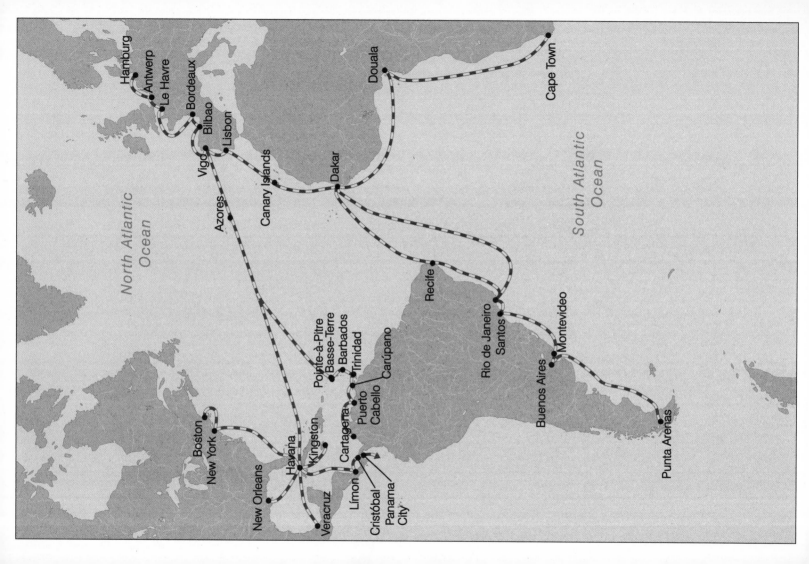

152 | Fine weather and calm seas offer perfect conditions for a game of shuffleboard on the deck of the Norddeutscher Lloyd liner *Columbus*.

155 | Passengers come ashore at Dakar from the *Africa* of the Compagnie des Chargeurs Réunis.

By the late nineteenth century, the Strait of Gibraltar was crowded with maritime traffic plying a number of the great sea routes that enabled shipping lines—not only from Mediterranean ports but also from all over Europe—to reach the West Indies, Central America, Mexico, and the United States, not forgetting the coastal towns of South America. Nor was this all: West Africa was served mainly by the French Chargeurs Réunis line, which in 1900 made ports of call at Dakar, the capital of Senegal, Conakry in western Guinea, Abidjan and Grand-Bassam in the Ivory Coast, and Cotonou in Benin. After World War II, the line operated its magnificent liners *Foucauld*, *Brazza*, and *Général Leclerc* from Bordeaux, where they would need to pass through the strait on an extended route to Douala in Cameroon, Libreville in Gabon, and Pointe-Noire in Guadeloupe.

In Central America, fierce competition raged between the lines as their routes extended westward, via the Panama Canal, to the United States, South America, Japan, the Pacific Ocean, and Australia. Before the 1930s, the West Indies were relatively neglected, apart from a few French and British steamers that supplied the islands. In 1931, the French Line operated the liner *Colombie* on the route from Le Havre to Southampton, Vigo, Pointe-à-Pitre,

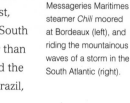

156 & 157 | The Messageries Maritimes steamer *Chili* moored at Bordeaux (left), and riding the mountainous waves of a storm in the South Atlantic (right).

Fort-de-France, Barbados, and Trinidad. Closed during the war, the route was reopened on October 12, 1950 with a modernized *Colombie*. From 1947, the *Corinthic, Athenic, Gothic, Ceramic, Southern Cross,* and *Northern Star* of the Shaw Savill Line made port call at Curaçao or Trinidad before navigating the Panama Canal. In the late 1960s, cruise operators made the Caribbean one of their most popular destinations, and have brought increasingly colossal ships into service, such as the 1996 launch of Carnival Cruise Lines' *Carnival Destiny,* larger than the QE2 and capable of holding more than 3,000 passengers and 1,000 staff.

Although the opening of the Suez Canal in 1869 had suddenly opened up faster and easier routes to the East, the volume of commercial trade between Europe and South America remained at a level almost three times higher than with the Far East. Yet the distances were immense, and the journey times interminable: seventeen days to reach Brazil, and twenty-three to make landfall in Argentina.

Spanish shipping lines were naturally among the first to operate routes to Latin America. In 1889, the Compañía Trasatlántica Española started services from Marseille to Buenos Aires via Barcelona, and from Barcelona to Havana and Vera Cruz, using liners of relatively low tonnage that could accommodate some 250 passengers in three classes and with considerable comfort. After World War I, the Ybarra Line offered routes to Bilbao, Montevideo, and Buenos Aires, initially on small ships and later on larger vessels.

Traffic on these routes remained heavy until the Spanish Civil War (1936–39), when services from the Iberian peninsula were suspended, to be resumed only in 1956, and then only for a few years. In 1903, Frederick Alcock, general manager of the Pacific Steam Navigation Company, listed no fewer than fifty-eight connections

157

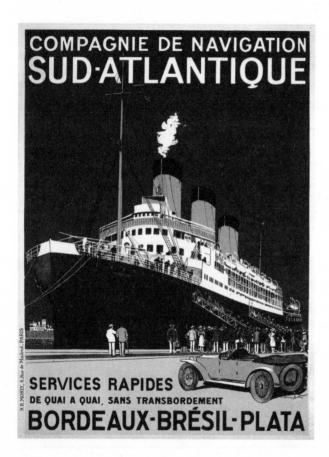

158

between Europe and South America, most of them fortnightly. Even counting only the mail boats, there were still twelve companies operating from Liverpool, Southampton, Hamburg, Bremen, Antwerp, Le Havre, St Nazaire, Bordeaux, Barcelona, Genoa, and Marseille.

At this time, South America was served by two British lines: the Pacific Steam Navigation Company and the Royal Mail Steam Packet Company; four French: Messageries Maritimes, Chargeurs Réunis, the Société Générale de Transports Maritimes à Vapeur, and the Compagnie Générale Transatlantique; three Italian: Navigazione Generale Italiana, Veloce, and Ligure Braziliana; and three German: Hamburg Amerika Linie, Norddeutscher Lloyd, and Kosmos.

All these vessels, steam-packets included, took on board large quantities of cargo, hence the number of intermediate ports of call on their routes. As Frederick Alcock wrote in his 1903 book *Trade & Travel in South America*, when the Pacific Steam Navigation Company's *Oropesa*, a liner carrying passengers divided into three classes, left port at Liverpool, she made first for La Rochelle. While she was being loaded with cargo, Alcock took the passengers ashore for a rapid guided tour of the town. Then she called in at A Coruña and Vigo, followed by

158 | A poster from the 1930s advertising the Compagnie de Navigation Sud-Atlantique offering service from Bordeaux to Brazil and Argentina.

159 | Havana was an important tourist port of call, as indicated by its covered piers, even at this early date c. 1910.

160

THE ROYAL MAIL STEAM PACKET COMPANY

Steamer _____ *Class* _____

Embarked _____

RIO.

Berth No. _____ *Name* _____

PASSENGERS' BAGGAGE.

160 | Crossing the line (the equator) was always an excuse for eccentric festivities, such as this procession aboard the Hapag liner *Resolute*.

161 | Passengers playing shuffleboard in a covered area on board a small American liner, c.1940.

the Portuguese ports of Leixões and Lisbon. At St. Vincent in the Cape Verde Islands she refueled with coal. Crossing the South Atlantic took five days, during which passengers found whatever means they could to pass the time. While some organized games of cricket on the promenade deck, others took advantage of the well-stocked library on board. As the sea air could be relied upon to whet appetites, mealtime was looked forward to, as Alcock wrote:

> Meal times on board ship are usually regarded as the events of the day, and the interest taken in them is generally enhanced by contact with our fellow passengers. There is the interchange of thoughts and opinions, the sharpening of one

mind by contact with another, and the never failing and appreciated anecdote or reminiscence, which serves to pass a pleasant hour or more. Then there is the study of character, always interesting, and more easily followed at dinner time than possibly any other, when minds expand and open under the genial influences of pleasant fare and good company.

Even on an unassuming liner such as the *Oropesa*, the service in first and second class was the equal of a restaurant of the highest quality. The catering arrangements in third class were perhaps less refined, but the helpings were equally enormous.

Whether for cases of seasickness or indigestion, the ship's doctor was much in demand and needed a good bedside manner. The favored remedy, much in vogue at the time, was to bind the stomach with a long strip of canvas. In 1907, doctors advised patients to "hold a hot-water compress, as hot as they can bear, to the head. This will produce a rush of blood to the head, so avoiding any depression of the brain." The professional advice of the crew, meanwhile, was to sail on a full stomach.

Each of these crossings was marked by a special event: passing the Equator, known as Crossing the Line. For this ceremony, a crewmember dressed as Neptune, with a false

beard and trident, would make a speech, after which all those who were Crossing the Line for the first time would be given a good soaking. King Neptune would then present each of them with a certificate of baptism. This exuberant ceremony took place in calm subtropical seas, the Horse Latitudes, whose name supposedly derives from the days when sailing ships might find themselves becalmed, and unfortunate horses on board would be thrown overboard as supplies of water and fodder ran low.

When the *Oropesa* arrived within view of Recife, in the Brazilian state of Pernambuco, passengers wishing to disembark were transferred onto a whaling boat. They had only a few hours to explore the town; soon a long blast on the ship's siren would summon everyone back on board. En route to Bahia, the ship passed a school of whales, and passengers hurried on deck to admire the spectacle. The ship's arrival at the breathtaking port of Rio de Janeiro was greeted with inclement weather, as Alcock wrote:

Unfortunately, the day upon which we arrived in Rio Bay was misty, and what may justly be termed one of the finest views in the world was spoilt. But we saw it later with the advantage of a clear sky and brilliant sunshine, and were convinced that all which has been written respecting this "miniature summer sea, upon whose bosom rest a hundred fairy isles, and around whose shores dimple a hundred bays," can but imperfectly describe its beauty. The surrounding mountains are clad in tropical verdure, and with the ever-changing hues of sky and mist, present a picture of incomparable beauty. The harbor is one of the largest and safest in the world, and the entrance, which is about a mile in width, is from a southerly direction, with the islands of Pai and Mai on the right, and Ihla Raza (with its lighthouse) and a number of other semibarren islands on the left. The entrance to the harbor is overlooked by the Sugar Loaf Mountain, and the coastline forms a huge resemblance of the human figure, and has thus come to be named the "Sleeping Giant."

The *Oropesa* spent forty-eight hours in Rio, unloading her cargo, reloading, and taking on supplies of coal. The passengers, meanwhile, set off to discover the city, and Alcock declared his delight at managing to visit Paqueta Island. Then the ship headed for Montevideo, where she spent another two days, before crossing the estuary of the Rio de La Plata to reach Buenos Aires; then it was on to the Falkland Islands and the west coast of South America.

In 1909, the Frenchman Edmond Garnier made the same voyage aboard the *Chili*, operated by Messageries Maritimes. Once on board, he was considerably less well pleased than Alcock, complaining at length about the lifeboats that blocked his view of the sea: "We are imprisoned between a wall of metal and the hulls of the lifeboats." In this he was echoing a common complaint of the time: perhaps this was the reason why the White Star Line decided not to increase the number of lifeboats on the *Titanic*?

The lifeboats were cumbersome not only to look at, but also to maneuver. In October 1927, when the *Principessa Mafalda*, a liner of the Italian Compania de Navigazione Generale, sank off Brazil as the result of damage to its engine, the inexperience of the crew in charge of launching and handling the lifeboats caused a chapter of accidents, so that despite the rapid arrival of several ships to take survivors on board, some 250 lives were lost. But generally speaking, there were fewer disasters on the South Atlantic crossings than on North Atlantic routes, partly because the ocean liners heading for Latin America were not constantly trying to outdo each other in speed, and partly because collisions were a less frequent occurrence.

Accidents did happen, however, and still do, even today. On November 23, 2007, the Liberian-registered cruise ship *Explorer* operated by the Canadian cruise company G.A.P. Adventures, was on a collision course with an iceberg some fifty miles off Antarctica. It was thirty-four minutes past midnight, and no one had realized the danger posed by the iceberg as it hove into view. At the moment of impact, the Swedish Captain Bengt Witman thought that the ship had hit a whale, and there was nothing to worry about. Unfortunately, the ship's hull had been gashed below the water line, and water rushed into the holds. As the ship developed a pronounced list to starboard, Witman sent out a mayday call and gave the order to abandon ship. An atmosphere of calm reigned as the eight semirigid lifeboats and six life rafts were launched, and everyone took their places in them. At about six in the morning the Norwegian ship *NordNorge*, the first to respond to the distress signals, arrived on the scene, and immediately took on board the hundred passengers and fifty-four crew of the *Explorer*. The ship finally sank at three thirty that afternoon, causing material damage only.

169 | At Dakar, the Navigazione Generale Italiana steamer *Principessa Mafalda*, enters floating dock for repairs. The port of Dakar was remarkably well equipped, as it was an important port of call for ships en route for Africa or South America. On October 25, 1927, the ship sank off the coast of Brazil after losing her propeller and an ensuing boiler explosion.

170 | Around 1930, a crowd throngs the dockside at Douala in Cameroon to watch the arrival of a Chargeurs Réunis mail steamer—the sole link between the colony and mainland France and the bearer of eagerly awaited letters and packets.

171 Left | An advertising brochure produced by the American travel agent Raymond & Whitcomb for a "Round Africa Cruise" on the *Carinthia* in 1929. Launched only four years earlier, on February 4, 1925, the *Carinthia* was a sumptuously appointed liner designed for the prestigious New York–Liverpool crossing.

171 Right | Smoking room on the Chargeurs Réunis liner *Asie*. While not actually banned from this bastion of masculine pastimes, female passengers were strongly discouraged from entering its portals. The emancipation of women might have made great strides during the inter-war period, but few members of the fairer sex were bold enough to smoke in public.

172–73 | After the opening of the Suez Canal, Cape Town lost some of its commercial importance but nevertheless remained a major port of call for cruise ships. Passengers have reboarded this liner after visiting the city, and now she is steaming off to another African port, or perhaps to South America.

174 Left | A 1932 publicity photograph by the A. Testa studio in Genoa for the Italian liner *Conte Biancamano* of the Flotte Riunite, a shipping line set up in 1931 with the sponsorship of Mussolini. Launched in 1925 by Lloyd Sabaudo, the *Conte Biancamano* was longer than her predecessors at 650 feet (198 meters), and boasted eight decks, five of them continuous; three swimming pools; and a wide array of sports amenities. Initially put into service to the Genoa–Naples–New York route, she was transferred to the South American crossing after the giant liners *Rex* and *Conte di Savoia* came into service.

Traveling at sea for the first time is a chance to realize that the ocean is not one ocean. The water changes. The Atlantic that seethes off the eastern United States is glaucous and lightless and looks mean. Around Jamaica, though, it's more like a milky aquamarine. Off the Cayman Islands it's an electric blue, and off Cozumel it's almost purple. Same deal with the beaches. You can tell right away that south Florida's sand comes from rocks: it hurts your bare feet and has that sort of mineralish glitter to it. But Ocho Rios's beach is more like dirty sugar, and Cozumel's is like clean sugar, and at places along the coast of Grand Cayman the sand's texture is more like flour, silicate, its white as dreamy and vaporous as clouds' white. The only real constant to the nautical topography of the Nadir's Caribbean is its unreal and almost retouched-looking prettiness. It's impossible to describe right; the closest I can come is to say that it all looks: expensive.

DAVID FOSTER WALLACE,

aboard the *Zenith* (which he called the *Nadir*), 1995

174 Right | A Hapag advertisement for its South American cruises, aimed at the line's American clientele, c.1910. With its close relations with several South American countries, Germany was particularly well placed to exploit this market.

175 | A liner in the Great Sound, Bermuda. After World War I, the British-owned Furness Bermuda Line (formerly the Quebec Steamship Company) made the British overseas territory of Bermuda a major tourist destination. The Prohibition era had a direct effect on tourism here, as wealthy Americans and rum runners came to the hotels of St. George and Hamilton, as well as to the cruise ships anchored off the islands, in search of liquor.

176 & 177 | On the upper deck of the Canadian Pacific's *Empress of Australia*, a steward offers refreshing drinks to a group of stylish young passengers, c.1934. In the gymnasium, meanwhile, a trio of young athletes demonstrates their prowess to three admiring young ladies.

177 Right | Luggage labels of the United Fruit Company, or Great White Fleet, a banana company that operated eleven steamers under the Honduran flag. Putting out of American east coast ports, they served the Caribbean, Central America, and Colombia.

178 | With the *Empress of Australia* still a few days' sail from Kingston, Jamaica (right), a bevy of young passengers (left) work on their suntans. A sports instructor is at hand to ensure that none of them succumbs to sunburn or, worse, sunstroke, c.1934.

179 | Nassau, capital of the Bahamas, lies on New Providence Island, which is linked to Paradise Island. Its magnificent harbor was formerly a favored haunt of pirates including the notorious English pirate Edward Teach, better known as Blackbeard. Nowadays, Nassau is a popular port of call for the largest cruise ships. The city has preserved many of its colonial style houses, its churches, and its eighteenth-century fortifications.

180–81 | Before the 1959 revolution, Cuba was a highly popular holiday destination for American tourists. *Who's Who Among Visitors to Havana and What's What in Cuba* (left), was essential reading for American passengers on board the *Transylvania*, bound for Nassau and Havana from New York in April 1938. On April 21, the sports instructor Jack Donovan improvised a boxing exhibition (center) by members of the crew on the promenade deck. A daily program from the cruise (right) shows the food and entertainment options open to passengers.

182–83 | SS *Transylvania* entering Havana harbor. During the Prohibition era, between 1920 and 1933, thousands of Americans took advantage of their vacations to stock up on liquor. Facundo Bacardi, owner of the famous distillery that bore his name, even invited them to "come to Cuba to bathe in Bacardi rum." Before the 1959 revolution, Cuba offered a wealth of entertainments, fine restaurants, casinos, dance halls, pretty girls, sandy beaches, and turquoise seas. Today the port of Havana still welcomes large numbers of cruise ships.

184–85 | The Compagnie Générale Transatlantique liner *Antilles* came into service in 1953, when she and the *Flandre* were the largest French liners sailing to the West Indies and Central America. Cruising at speeds of up to 23 knots, they could make the voyage from Le Havre to Fort-de-France in seven days. In 1956, in response to passengers' complaints that smuts were dirtying their clothes, the funnel was raised by 10 feet (3 meters)—with the unexpected effect of improving the ship's lines. With her swimming pool, solarium, and mechanotherapy room, where a practitioner used specialized equipment to manipulate passengers' joints, the *Antilles* was extremely popular with tourists. From 1966 she operated trips to the Caribbean, with passengers returning to their point of departure by plane, a highly successful combination that was abruptly cut short on January 8, 1971, when she struck an uncharted reef on her way out to Barbados. With the shock of the collision some of her fuel caught fire, and the blaze quickly spread to the engine room. The captain gave the order to abandon ship, and passengers took refuge on the nearby island of Mustique. There were no casualties, but the *Antilles* could not be salvaged.

167

186 | The terrace of the Grand Salon aboard SS *Antilles*. Passengers would hardly know they were on an ocean liner.

187 | A stateroom with a porthole on a French liner. Tasteful and functional, it bears comparison with rooms in the best hotels on either side of the Atlantic at this period, and was fully air-conditioned, naturally.

188 | Crossing the Equator, known as crossing the line, was invariably an excuse for madcap celebrations, generally at the expense of those who had never crossed the line before. Here stewardesses' backs sport caricatures of the novices on board, in preparation for some arcane game in which they will inevitably be the losers. The scene takes place in 1937, during a world cruise by the Cunard liner *Franconia*.

189 | As SS *Franconia* crosses the line in 1937, two burly sailors guide a blindfolded young passenger towards a tub of water. His reward will be a certificate signed by Neptune, the lord of misrule, who presided over the festivities.

190 Left | A wide range of activities was offered on board with a view to fending off boredom. Here passengers duly throw themselves into a game of quoits on the promenade deck of the *Empress of Australia*.

190 Right | A Chargeurs Réunis poster, c.1930.

191 | The port of Santos, near Sao Paolo in Brazil, could accommodate very large ships; in the 1930s it was a popular port of call for ocean liners.

192 | A view of one of the world's most glorious beaches, Copacabana in Rio de Janeiro, from the terrace of the Copacabana Palace Hotel.

193 | Two great liners of the Flotte Riunite route between Genoa and Buenos Aires pass each other in mid-South Atlantic. Between 1857 and 1958, nearly half of all the immigrants to Argentina were from Italy, with over three million Italians settling there.

194 | The ship's band on an American liner in the 1940s serenades passengers as they arrive at Buenos Aires.

195 | The Messageries Maritimes pier at Buenos Aires in the 1930s. As most of the incoming vessels were mixed cargo and passenger ships, the docks here handled a considerable volume of freight. Most passengers traveling to Argentina at this period were intending either to settle or to do business.

196 | A Hamburg-Südamerikanische poster from the late 1920s. Following the total destruction of its fleet during World War I, this shipping line moved into chartering passenger liners. From 1924 it launched its Monte-class liners, classless steamers designed to carry immigrants to South America. On the *Monte Sarmiento*, for example, the price of cabins was on a sliding scale according to their position within the ship, but nowhere was out of bounds to third-class passengers. The vessel could accommodate 1006 passengers in cabins and 1456 on deck. As the number of immigrants to Brazil and Argentina dropped, the Monte-class liners began to specialize in charter cruises to Norway during the summer months. These early popular cruises, pioneers of mass tourism, paved the way for the creation in November 1933, under the Nazi regime, of the leisure and tourism organization Kraft durch Freude, which chartered the Monte-class liners of the Hamburg-Südamerikanische line on a regular basis.

197 | Landing stages at Montevideo, Uruguay, c.1890. The harbor bristles with merchant ships, mostly sporting sailing rigs. The scarcity of coal depots forced many shipping lines to keep their sailing vessels in service up to the end of World War I.

198–99 | Cruises to Antarctica from Chile and Argentina have proliferated since the 1970s. Here MS *Nordkap* of the Hurtigruten line is shown lying at anchor in Andvord Bay at Neko Harbor in Antarctica. With a bit of luck, her passengers who have disembarked on to the ice and rocks may enjoy a sighting of emperor penguins.

169

Round Africa
Cruise · 1929

P. B. PARSONS

RAYMOND & WHITCOMB CO.

ASIE. SALLE à MANGER

171

173

HAMBURG AMERICAN

CRUISES

"The last word in pleasure cruising"

The unusual facilities and comprehensive arrangements—the results of over 20 years' experience—and our fleet of splendidly appointed and equipped cruising steamships, assure our patrons of the very acme of convenience and luxurious comfort, at rates remarkably low for the services rendered.

Our program for the Winter season includes the

West Indies

3 Cruises by the magnificent S. S. MOLTKE (12,500 tons), the largest vessel ever sent to the Carribbean. 2 Cruises of 28 days and 1 Cruise of 16 days during January, February and March, 1910. Costs from $85 and $150 upwards. Visits to St. Thomas, Jamaica, Colon (Panama Canal), Venezuela, Trinidad, Martinique, Havana, Nassau, and Bermuda.

Also delightful trips on splendid "PRINZ" steamers of our Atlas Line at very attractive rates.

Cincinnati Orient Cruise

The finest and most attractive Orient Cruise ever scheduled.

The most comprehensive itinerary ever arranged, including twenty-one ports, along the Mediterranean, Egypt, the Nile, the Holy Land, the Orient, etc., covering over 15,000 miles. The longest Oriental Cruise ever scheduled. Eighty days, leaving New York January twenty-ninth.

The S. S. CINCINNATI, on which the Cruise is made, is one of the finest steamers afloat—ideally adapted for the purpose, and equipped with every convenience and luxury.

Cost $325 and up including landing and embarking expenses

South America *including the* Straits of Magellan

BRAZIL, ARGENTINA, URUGUAY and CHILE—duration 81 days

Overland trips across the Cordilleras of the Andes to Valparaiso and Santiago de Chile, and visits to the magnificent Fjords of the Straits of Magellan.

By the Twin-Screw S. S. "BLEUCHER" (12,500 tons). Leaving New York January 22, 1910. Cost from $350 upward

We have issued a series of "Travel Books" describing these Cruises, giving full particulars, which will be sent on application

HAMBURG AMERICAN LINE, 41-45 Broadway, New York

BOSTON   PHILADELPHIA   CHICAGO   ST. LOUIS   SAN FRANCISCO

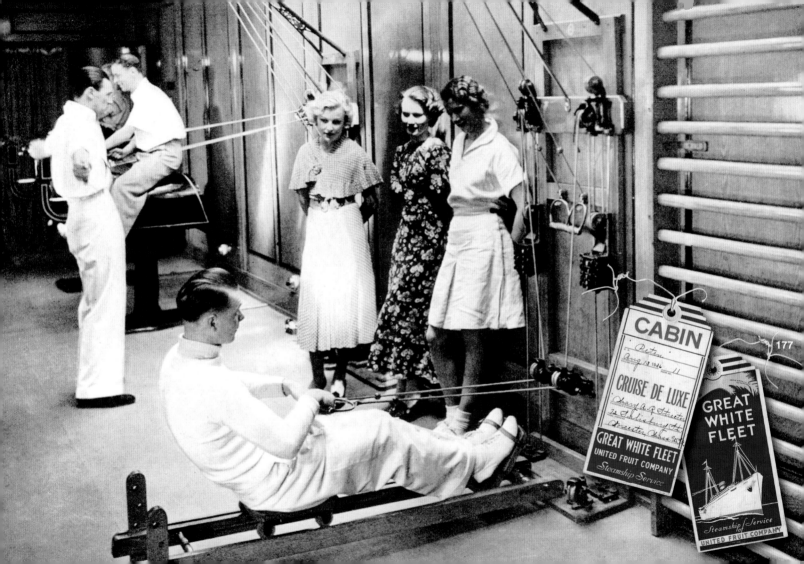

178

179

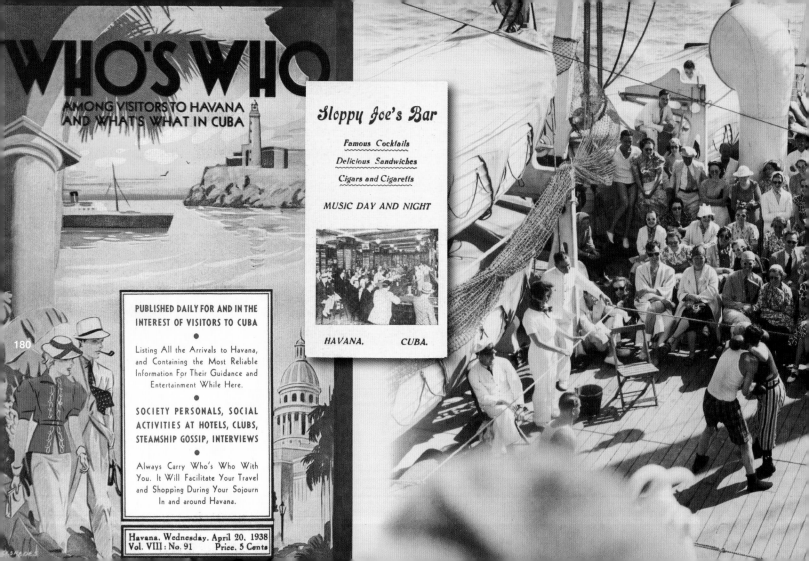

WHO'S WHO

AMONG VISITORS TO HAVANA AND WHAT'S WHAT IN CUBA

Sloppy Joe's Bar

Famous Cocktails

Delicious Sandwiches

Cigars and Cigarettes

MUSIC DAY AND NIGHT

HAVANA.   CUBA.

PUBLISHED DAILY FOR AND IN THE INTEREST OF VISITORS TO CUBA

•

Listing All the Arrivals to Havana, and Containing the Most Reliable Information For Their Guidance and Entertainment While Here.

SOCIETY PERSONALS, SOCIAL ACTIVITIES AT HOTELS, CLUBS, STEAMSHIP GOSSIP, INTERVIEWS

Always Carry Who's Who With You. It Will Facilitate Your Travel and Shopping During Your Sojourn In and around Havana.

Havana, Wednesday, April 20, 1938
Vol. VIII : No. 91   Price. 5 Cents

ANCHOR LINE
NASSAU-HAVANA CRUISE

R.M.S. TRANSYLVANIA   Commander DAVID W. BONE

THURSDAY, APRIL 21, 1938

To-Day's Program

8.00 a.m.-10.00 a.m.   **Breakfast**

10.00 a.m.   **Morning Exercise,** Promenade deck Aft, conducted by Mr Jack Denovan, Gym Instructor

10.30 a.m.   **Ping Pong Tournament** (Gentlemen), A deck, Aft. Prizes. See Mr Dutton or Mr Gill

12 Noon.   **Buffet Luncheon,** A deck, Aft (weather permitting)

12 Noon.   **Lunch** (First Sitting), Dining Rooms, D deck

1.30 p.m.   **Lunch** (Second Sitting), Dining Rooms, D deck

3.00 p.m.   **Boxing Exhibition** by Members of the Crew, Promenade deck

4.00 p.m.   **Bridge Party,** Lounge, A deck Aft. Prizes

5.30 p.m.   **Cocktail Hour**—Tony and his Accordion, Smoke Room, A deck, Aft

6.15 p.m.   **Dinner** (First Sitting), Dining Rooms, D deck

7.30 p.m.   **Dinner** (Second Sitting), Dining Rooms, D deck

8.15 p.m.   **Movies**—"100 Men and a Girl," with Deanna Durbin, Leopold Stokowski and Adolphe Menjou, A deck, Aft

9.30 p.m.   **Repeat showing** of "100 Men and a Girl"

10.45 p.m.   **Dancing under the Stars,** Promenade deck

SPECIAL NOTICE

The Navigation Bridge will be open for Inspection between the hours of 10-11.30 a.m. 2-5 p.m.

COMING EVENT

To-Morrow, Friday, April 22, 1938. Fancy Dress Party
Prizes for the most Original, Artistic and Humorous Costumes. Let's have a grand turnout. Start working on your Costumes now. Masks, false faces, etc. may be purchased from Miss Raeside in the Shop on A Deck, Forward

JAMES BALLANTYNE, Cruise Director

NASSAU-HAVANA CRUISE
S.S. TRANSYLVANIA—NASSAU
Tender Schedule
FROM SHIP TO SHORE
8.30 a.m.   9.30 a.m.   10.30 a.m.   2 p.m.
FROM SHORE TO SHIP
12 Noon   3 p.m.   4 p.m.
Ship sails on embarkation from last tender
Kindly report to Bedroom Steward on return to Ship

183

187

190

BRÉSIL - PLATA
PAR LES COMPAGNIES DE NAVIGATION
CHARGEURS RÉUNIS
SUD - ATLANTIQUE

191

192

ITALIA

FLOTTE RIUNITE COSULICH · LLOYD SABAUDO · NAVIGAZ. GENERALE

Incontro in Oceano di due grandi piroscafi della Linea SUD AMERICA EXPRESS

193

197

THROUGH THE SUEZ CANAL
TO THE FAR EAST

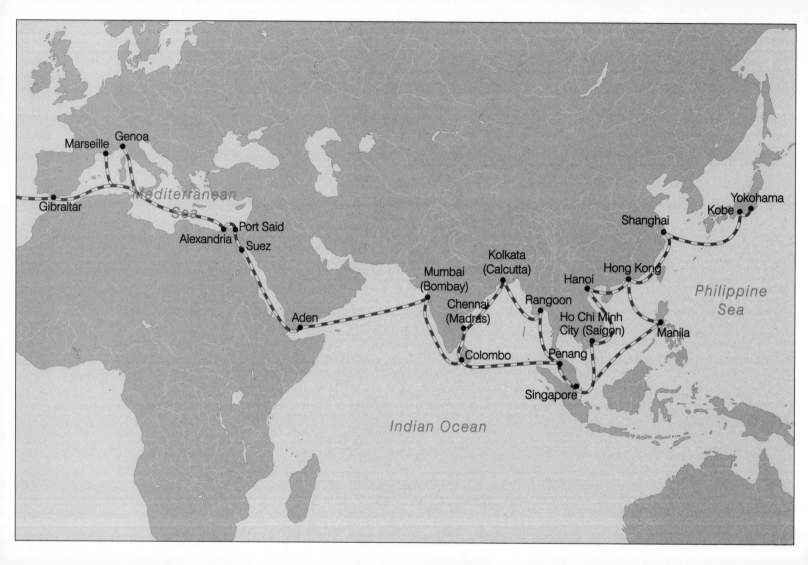

200 | A pair of Japanese pleasure trippers with their attendants in a rowboat gaze at the *König Albert* in this Norddeutscher Lloyd poster advertising routes to the Far East via Suez, c.1900.

203 | A postcard of Brindisi.

On October 2, 1872, at 8:45 in the evening, Phileas Fogg left London by train. The following day, he caught another train from Paris to Turin, via the Mont Cenis railway tunnel, which had opened for traffic in September 1871. From Turin he traveled on to Brindisi, where he immediately embarked on the *Mongolia*, a steamer of the celebrated P&O Company that offered regular service to Bombay via Suez. Thus begins Jules Verne's *Around the World in Eighty Days*, first published in 1873, in which the hero puts the efficiency of the world's new railway and maritime connections to the test, on the way steaming through the Suez Canal, opened just three years before his famous journey, in 1869.

Even before the construction of the modern canal, the Suez route had enabled Europeans to reach Asia without rounding the Cape of Good Hope. The P&O (the Peninsular and Oriental Steam Navigation Company)—effectively founded in 1837, when it won the British Admiralty mail concession for India, and incorporated by royal charter in 1840—operated a route between Suez and Calcutta from 1843. Regular contact was thus assured between Britain and her vast empire before the idea of a canal became a reality. P&O steam-packets would sail via Gibraltar to Alexandria, where they off-loaded post and passengers for a grueling overland expedition. The first leg of the journey was by river, on small and far from comfortable vessels. Then the hardy travelers crossed the desert by diligence to Suez, where another steamer waited to take them on to India. The journey from Alexandria to Suez took some twenty-eight hours, though with the opening of the Alexandria–Suez railway in December 1858 matters improved somewhat. This slow and laborious transfer did not, however, prevent P&O from extending its postal service to Hong Kong in 1845, starting a fortnightly steam-packet between Singapore and Australia in 1852, and extending its lines to Japan in 1859.

P&O was not the only shipping company to cross the isthmus at Suez by land. Under a blazing sun, its expeditions would sometimes encounter convoys of passengers and post under the auspices of the French Messageries Maritimes. In 1861, ten years after its creation, this steam-packet company (state-sponsored like P&O) was entrusted with a new service to China, with a transfer via Suez. The line was inaugurated by the liner *Impératrice*, recently launched at the company's Mediterranean shipyards at La Ciotat in the presence of Napoleon III. France relied on Oriental imports for its industries (notably for silk), and hoped also to reopen its old trading route to India (where it still had five small trading posts), while at the same time confirming the highly promising French presence in Cochin China. The creation of this regular service was thus dictated as much by economic necessity as by political concerns. From 1865, Messageries Maritimes also extended its service to Japan.

Other European shipping lines, such as Rotterdam Lloyd (founded in 1839), continued to follow the traditional route around the Cape of Good Hope, even after the inauguration of the Suez Canal. Indeed, until 1872, when it launched a steamer service between Amsterdam and Batavia in Indonesia, Rotterdam Lloyd's routes to the Dutch East Indies were operated only by sailing ships. It should not be forgotten, moreover, that until the late nineteenth century sailing ships carried out some 50 percent of the world's maritime trade, at least on traditional routes, but when the Suez Canal was finally opened in November 1869, it was navigable only by steamships.

Britain had for many years been hostile to building the Suez Canal, fearing the threat of foreign intrusion on its route to the Indies. An outcry in the British press about the conditions of the forced Egyptian labor being used for the excavations succeeded in stopping work for several months (despite Britain's own questionable colonial labor practices).

205 | The entrance to the Suez Canal. Moored at the quayside are houseboats to accommodate the engineers and technicians working on the canal, alongside dredgers.

206 | It was here at Port Said that canal pilots boarded ships arriving from the Mediterranean.

When work started again, the Egyptian workers were duly rewarded. And the advantages offered by the canal soon mollified any objections. Before, with the overland transfer, the journey from Europe to Hong Kong had taken some six weeks; now it took a month or less. By 1874, no less then 74 percent of ships using the canal were British, with the French accounting for a mere 9 percent.

It became clear that in order to compensate for obvious imbalances and offer the public a coordinated service, the various shipping companies would have to come to an understanding among themselves—and all the more so given that globally they exploited the same lines and followed the same routes. Thus it was that P&O and Messageries Maritimes signed an agreement to their mutual advantage, by which they alternated their scheduled departures. And on a broader scale, there were also conferences aimed at regulating international trade.

Most histories of ocean liners tend to focus principally on the passenger trade, yet the freight trade for these mail companies was highly lucrative, if a touch specialized. Steamships could not afford to carry heavy cargo as well as fuel, so until the end of the nineteenth century heavy and bulky merchandise was shipped under sail. In the years after the opening of the canal, steam-packets on Asian routes tended to carry expensive luxury products, such as Paris perfumes, wine, and watches—not to mention banknotes and coins for the colonies and other client states, a remunerative if high-security cargo. On the return journey, the ships' holds would be stocked with exotic and sometimes surprising cargoes: Semiluxury supplies such as cinnamon, pepper, gum Arabic, rice, and medicinal plants would be supplemented by opium, which at this time was freely on sale in French Indochina. Sometimes the holds would be filled with whole menageries of wild animals on their way to European zoos. And sometimes the ships' merchandise would be on its way to one of Europe's great museums: when the Messageries Maritimes steamer *Meikong* foundered off Yemen's port of Aden in 1877, it had statues from Angkor Wat on board. Prominent among these valuable cargoes were boxes of silkworm cocoons for the silk manufacturers of Lyon and Italy, as well as gorgeous lengths of silk taken on board in Hong Kong or Yokohama. Indeed, the mail companies operated a monopoly of sorts in the export of silks, precisely because of the regularity and reliability of the service they offered.

To regulate this traffic and define minimum cargo rates, the various shipping companies needed to organize conferences. The French historian Marie-Françoise Berneron-Couvenhes has documented the first of these, in 1879, attended by five British shipping companies and one French, Messageries Maritimes. At later conferences, however, newcomers active on the routes to the East appeared—most notably, from the 1890s, German and Japanese companies such as Norddeutscher Lloyd in 1893 and Nippon Yusen Kaisha in 1896.

Competition raged most fiercely in the passenger trade. In the 1880s, P&O started offering special rates for large families (enlarged even further by their servants, who accompanied them). The German lines, meanwhile, offered free passage to all officials from the Chinese and Japanese embassies, hoping that they would ensure them good publicity among their fellow countrymen and discourage them from traveling on rival lines. Finally, as on all other routes, rival companies vaunted the quality of their accommodations, the elegance of their appointments, and the quality of their catering (an important consideration on a voyage lasting several weeks).

But who were these passengers bound for the Orient? There was no mass immigration as on the transatlantic lines, so the numbers of steerage, or third class, passengers were much smaller than on other routes. On the other hand, Muslims from the Malay states on pilgrimage to Mecca offered a relatively lucrative alternative. In *Lord Jim*, published in 1900, Joseph Conrad described the multitudes of poor pilgrims who crowded onto these steamships, and the terrible risks they sometimes ran. Conrad wrote:

> After [the ship *Patna*] had been painted outside and whitewashed inside, eight hundred pilgrims (more or less) were driven on board of her as she lay with steam up alongside a wooden jetty. They streamed aboard over three gangways, they streamed in urged by faith and the hope of paradise, they streamed in with a continuous tramp and shuffle of bare feet, without a word, a murmur, or a look back; and when clear of confining rails spread on all sides over the deck, flowed forward and aft, overflowed down the yawning hatchways, filled the inner recesses of the ship—like water filling a cistern, like water flowing into crevices and crannies, like water rising silently even with the rim. Eight hundred men and women with faith and hopes, with affections and memories, they had collected there, coming from north and south and from the outskirts of the East, after treading the jungle paths, descending the rivers, coasting in *praus* along the shallows, crossing in small canoes from island to island, passing through suffering, meeting strange sights, beset by strange fears, upheld by one desire.

Conrad's tale, based on true events of the abandonment of a sinking steamer full of pilgrims, was a particularly shocking example. The steam-packets, however, having by definition to observe a fixed itinerary, were not able to take full advantage of the requirements of this sort of clientele. P&O and Messageries Maritimes both found themselves obliged to put pilgrims ashore at Aden or Suez, both a very long way from Mecca. Independent steamers, though sometimes riskier, offered the advantage of being able to put in at the much closer port of Jeddah.

The passengers on board the steam-packets on these routes, whether in first class or steerage, were a motley and colorful crew. They had one thing in common, however: Here as elsewhere, until the 1920s at least, virtually all passengers were on board through necessity, for professional or business reasons, or to try their luck in some remote clime. Every aspect of colonial life and bureaucracy was represented, including brokers, planters, functionaries from French Indochina, officers traveling on official

209 | Despite the stifling heat of Port Said, the strict codes of etiquette in force on board required that passengers should dress as though in town.

208

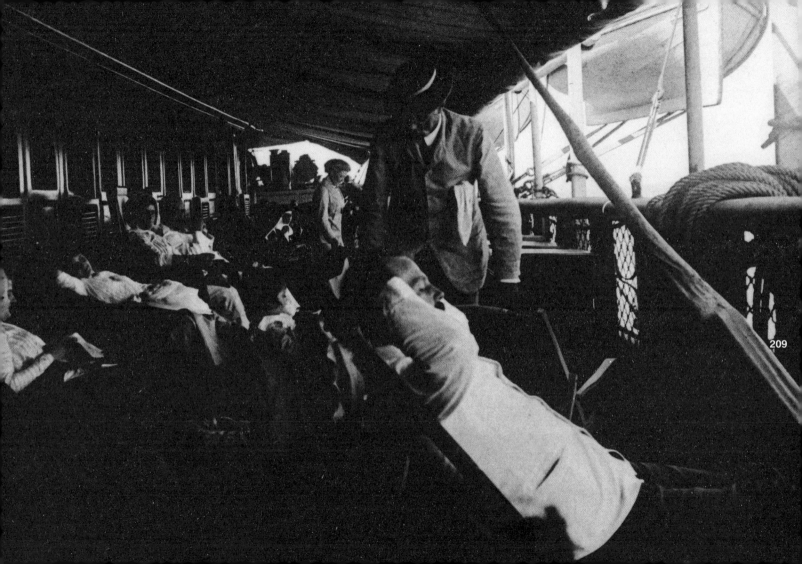

209

210 | Taking on coal in Port Said: Under a scorching sun, hundreds of workers toil up and down the gangway, bowed under the weight of large wicker baskets filled with coal from the barge in the foreground.

211 | Lying at anchor in the waters off Aden, ships await the barges that will deliver their cargo and the boats that will ferry out their passengers.

business, adventurers, archaeologists, animal hunters commissioned by zoos, missionaries, and British administrators returning to Bombay after their five-yearly leave. Added to these were a few wealthy eccentrics, tourists traveling in groups under the auspices of the first tour operators, and theatrical troupes setting off on tour to Hanoi or Saigon. Altogether they offered a picturesque and idiosyncratic cast of characters, offering rich inspiration to novelists and helping to create the legendary reputation of these Oriental routes. And the very nature of the voyages—long and slow, with so many different legs and exotic ports of call—added to their glamour.

For decades after the opening of the Suez Canal, the itineraries of these leisurely cruises remained unchanged, and were accompanied by rituals that passengers passed on from generation to generation.

In Port Said—the first port of call on the route to the Indies from London, Marseille, or Brindisi—while the ship

took on coal, the passengers would set off to buy a few souvenirs, or perhaps a pith helmet if they had forgotten to bring one. Then they would spend a day on the canal: terribly long and monotonous, except for the pink pelicans that the guide would point out at the Bitter Lakes. As a rule, to kill time the passengers would all change here, unanimously adopting white linen. Then came the Red Sea: the temperature would continue rising, the heat becoming insufferable. From this point on, the decks would be hung with grayish awnings and watered regularly; at night, passengers would abandon their stifling cabins to sleep outside on deckchairs. Finally there was the blistering heat of Aden and Djibouti, where there wasn't much to see, apart from the spectacle of beggar children diving for coins from small open boats. As the ship steamed into the Indian Ocean, the passengers were able breathe again at last. Some vessels, mostly British, then headed north for Bombay. The rest carried on to Ceylon (present-day Sri Lanka), one of the most eagerly anticipated ports of call. Passengers would stand on deck, scanning the horizon for their first sight of it, some of them having heard that you could smell its spice-laden perfumes before you could see it.

212 | Dwarfed by the flank of a steamer at anchor, fishermen in their outriggers wait to row passengers ashore at Colombo in Sri Lanka.

213 | P&O passengers from Europe pick their way down the gangway in an Indian port, probably Calcutta (now Kolkata), c.1910. A train is standing by to carry them into the interior.

At Colombo, the capital of Ceylon and the world's crossroads, routes separated again. Some steamers headed south for Australia, others north for Calcutta or Rangoon. But most of them headed across the Gulf of Bengal and through the Malacca Straits for their next port of call: Singapore. Many British passengers disembarked here. Dutch passengers went on to the Indonesian ports of Batavia (present-day Jakarta) or Surabaya. French passengers went farther, to Vietnam's Saigon, Hué, or Hanoi. By the time the steamers entered the choppy gray waters of the China Sea they were already virtually empty. Still on board were passengers for Hong Kong, Shanghai, and last of all, the handful bound for Yokohama, Japan, the final port of call on this long voyage.

These journeys were to continue practically unchanged, impervious to all international conflicts and colonial independence, until the Six Days War in 1967, when the Suez Canal was closed. It was not to open again until 1974, by which time the world had changed. Messageries Maritimes had merged with Transat; and P&O had diversified its activities, turning to the cruise market and investing in a variety of airlines—including Cathay Pacific, which now serves Hong Kong.

214 | By the end of the nineteenth century, Singapore was equipped to handle the great mail steamers en route to the Far East.

215 | As a steamer comes in to dock at Hong Kong around 1930, Chinese street peddlers crowd the quayside to tempt them with their wares: local handiwork, postcards, and maps of the city.

216 | American tourists unloading in the port of Yokohama, about 1910.

Mrs. Hamlyn lay on her long chair and lazily watched the passengers come along the gangway. The ship had reached Singapore in the night, and since dawn had been taking on cargo; the winches had been grinding away all day, but by now her ears were accustomed to their insistent clamor. She had lunched at the Europe, and for lack of anything better to do had driven in a rickshaw through the gay, multitudinous streets of the city. Singapore is the meeting-place of many races. The Malays, though natives of the soil, dwell uneasily in towns, and are few; and it is the Chinese, supple, alert, and industrious, who throng the streets; the dark-skinned Tamils walk on their silent, naked feet, as though they were but brief sojourners in a strange land, but the Bengalis, sleek and prosperous, are easy in their surroundings, and self-assured; the sly and obsequious Japanese seem busy with pressing and secret affairs; and the English in their topees and white ducks, speeding past in motor-cars or at leisure in their rickshaws, wear a nonchalant and careless air. The rulers of these teeming peoples take their authority with smiling unconcern. And now, tired and hot, Mrs. Hamlyn waited for the ship to set out again on her long journey across the Indian Ocean.

W. SOMERSET MAUGHAM, "P & O," 1926

The canal has prospered beyond the dreams of its author; but this means no more to the country through which it runs than the success of the canals of Mars. De Lesseps died in a madhouse and practically a pauper . . . These are but some of the tragic side-lights of the great story of the Suez Canal. . . . there was a movement in France to perpetuate De Lesseps's name by officially calling the waterway the Canal de Lesseps. But . . . as a modified measure, the canal administration was willing to appropriate a modest sum to provide a statue of the once honored man to be placed at the Mediterranean entrance of the canal.

There stands today on the jetty at Port Said, consequently, a bronze effigy of the man for a few years known as *"Le grand Français,"* visage directed toward Constantinople (where once he had been potent in intrigue), the left hand holding a map of the canal, while the right is raised in graceful invitation to the maritime world to enter . . . In Cairo and Alexandria it is flippantly said that De Lesseps traced with his gold-headed walking-stick the course of the canal in the sand, while hundreds of thousands of unpaid natives scooped the soil out with their hands. The work was completed with dredges and labor-saving machinery, as a fact. The enterprise cost practically $100,000,000—a million dollars a mile; and half this was employed in greasing the wheels at Constantinople and Paris.

FREDERIC COURTLAND PENFIELD, East of Suez: Ceylon, Indian, China and Japan, 1907

The passage of the Suez Canal is interesting only on one of the large steamers, for from the small steamboats which ply regularly between [Ismailia and Port Said] the passenger cannot see beyond the embankments of the Canal. The S. part of the Canal, from [Ismailia] to Suez, is the more interesting. The passage from [Port Said] to Suez occupies 15–22 hrs. The fare by the British steamers is about 3p., by the French steamers 100 fr., by the German steamers 44–60 marks; [plus] the tax levied by the Canal Co. on each traveler . . .

KARL BAEDECKER, ED., *Egypt*, 1902

On the 13th the *Carnatic* entered Yokohama harbor on the morning tide.

Yokohama is an important stopping-off point in the Pacific, used by all the steamers that transport mail and passengers between North America, China, Japan, and Malaya. Yokohama is situated in Tokyo Bay, quite close to that enormous town, which is the second capital of the Japanese empire and where the Shogun used to live in the days when this title of civil emperor existed. Tokyo is also the rival of Kyoto, the great city where the Mikado, the holy emperor descended from the gods, lives.

The *Carnatic* docked in Yokohama, near the jetties of the port and the customs sheds, amid a large number of ships from all over the world. . . . Passepartout found himself to begin with in a truly European-style city, with houses with low facades, decorated with verandas beneath which spread elegant colonnades. Its streets, squares, docks, and wharves covered the whole area between the Treaty Promontory and the river. There, as in Hong Kong or Calcutta, was a swarming mass of people of all races, Americans, English, Chinese and Dutch, merchants prepared to buy and sell anything under the sun. Amid all these a French person would have looked as much of an outsider as if he'd been abandoned among savages.

JULES VERNE, Around the World in Eighty Days, 1873

The 1st of February found us halfway between Madras and Colombo. On the next, the blue hills of Ceylon were close on the "port bow," and some of the passengers affirmed that they could sniff the "spicy breezes" that blew off "Ceylon's Isle," but I was not so fortunate. All day we have been running in sight of that lovely island. . . . With the exception of Majorca, Ceylon has the loveliest line of hill and mountain that I have seen from sea—the nearer land green as an emerald, with distant hills fading into the ether. We entered the harbor of Colombo on the night of February 2, and landed next morning, rowed in by swarthy natives . . .

LORD RONALD GOWER,
aboard the P&O Steamer *Teheran*, February 1884

. . . In two days I'll be in Nouméa, where the boat for Tahiti will pick me up. The crossing was very smooth and rapid, with glorious weather—just for my benefit. But what a lot of extraordinary passengers [are] on these voyages. I am the only one paying for his passage. All of them are government employees— and the good, kind government pays for little jaunts for all these useless people, their wives and children, which add up. Basically they are very decent people who have only one fault, quite a common one for that matter, that of being altogether mediocre.

PAUL GAUGUIN, May 1891

225 | A P&O steamer sets sail for the Far East. From 1844, P&O operated a regular service from Southampton, and later London, to Alexandria, and from Suez to Ceylon, Madras, and Calcutta. From 1845 the route was extended to Penang, Singapore, Hong Kong, and Shanghai. Passengers here board the steamer accompanied by their numerous trunks and steamer bags heaped in piles on deck by an army of porters. First-class passengers such as these will spend much of the voyage changing into different outfits from their lavish wardrobes.

226–27 | The port of La Joliette, Marseille, c.1870. The opening of the Suez Canal in 1869 turned La Joliette into a major hub for sea traffic to India and the Far East. Moored in the foreground is a merchant sailing ship, almost certainly bound for a Mediterranean port with her cargo. Most of the other ships in harbor are steamers probably en route to the Suez Canal and the Red Sea.

228–29 | Life on board the P&O steamer *Himalaya*, bound for India from Southampton in the early 1890s, as depicted by W.W. Lloyd in his *P&O Pencillings*. "Mr Smith feels he might possibly survive another ten minutes," reads the caption to the dining room scene, "if his charming companion and the attentive stewards would leave him alone." The sailors on these routes, many from the Malabar Coast, were famed for their outstanding seamanship and iron constitutions.

230 | Poster by Jos Rovers depicting the SS *Patria* of the Royal Rotterdam Lloyd Line in around 1924, with her dummy second funnel. Built in 1919, the *Patria* was designed to accommodate 120 passengers in first class, 124 in second, 44 in third, and 44 in steerage. This Dutch company operated the Rotterdam-Suez-Batavia route for nearly 90 years, from 1872 to 1960, with ports of call at Southampton, Lisbon, Tangier, Gibraltar, Marseille, Port Said, Suez, Colombo, Sabang, Belawan, Singapore, and Surabaya.

231 | A steamer from the Mediterranean enters the Suez Canal. The jetty is crowded with feluccas, recognizable by their long lateen rigs, which Egyptian sailors maneuver with expert skill. In the middle distance, the statue of Ferdinand de Lesseps marks the entrance to the canal. Destroyed during the Suez Crisis of 1956 and restored only in 1987, the statue now stands on one of the quays at Port Fouad.

232 | Indian crewmembers of the cargo ship *Al Kahira*, operated by the Khedivial Mail Steamship & Graving Dock Company, pose for the camera with Port Said behind. Formed in 1898 to run the ships and warehouses of the various departments of the Egyptian government, this company was registered under the British flag, and carried cargo and passengers to Alexandria, Constantinople, the ports of Syria and the Red Sea, Piraeus, Malta, Marseille, and Cyprus. In the 1950s it opened up a route from Port Said to Bombay and Karachi.

233 | The waterfront and rue du Commerce in Port Said, c.1900. Built on sandbanks, Port Said owed its existence to the opening of the canal and enjoyed a dubious reputation, consisting almost exclusively of shady hotels and cafés frequented by sailors from the ships anchored in one of the port's three docks, interspersed with foreign exchange bureaus and seedy gambling joints of ill repute. "Beware of all gambling houses," warned the *Guide Madrolle* produced by the French Comité de l'Asie in 1902.

234 | Photochrom image of a cargo and passenger steamer of British India Associated Steamers in the Suez Canal, c.1900. Although they transported their passengers in conditions of comfort, these vessels could obviously not vie in speed with the mail steamers, and were put into service on routes where passenger numbers would not have been sufficient to justify the operation of larger ships. In the canal there was a speed limit of six knots for all ships, so that it took twenty hours to navigate its length.

235 | The Canadian Pacific Line's *Empress of Scotland* navigating the Suez Canal. Built in 1905 as the *Kaiserin Auguste Victoria* for the Hamburg Amerika Linie, at her launch this vessel was the largest ship in the world, measuring 675 feet (206 meters) in length and 78 feet (24 meters) in breadth. Captured by the Allies during World War I, she was ceded in February 1920 to Cunard, who sold her to Canadian Pacific. Following a cruise of the Mediterranean and Red Sea in 1922, she operated on North Atlantic routes.

236–37 | Bombay Harbor (now Mumbai Harbor), c.1900. This sheltered harbor was an anchorage of choice for vessels waiting to enter the constantly crowded port. At the turn of the century, Bombay was already India's second city, with a population of more than a million people.

238 | The harbor at Colombo was well protected from the ocean's swell by a breakwater, and negotiating the harbor entrance was by no means as difficult as it looked.

239 | Passengers being ferried from the Messageries Maritimes steamer *Indus* (1897–1916) to the port of Colombo in 1902. At this time mail steamers were unable to enter the harbor—even those of a length limited to 443 feet (135 meters) so that they could navigate the Saigon River. The second of the four *Laos* sister ships, the *Indus* began her career on routes to the Far East, before being transferred in 1903 to the Bordeaux–Buenos Aires route, and renamed *Magellan*. Returning to the Far East in 1912, she carried mail in the early years of World War I, before being converted into a troop carrier. In March and April 1915 she took part in the Dardanelles expedition, and on December 11, 1916 she was sunk by a German torpedo.

240 | Passengers on the deck of the Messageries Maritimes mail steamer *Tourane*, sister ship to the *Indus*, being lulled by the sea breezes. Launched on November 6, 1898 at La Ciotat, the *Annam*, as she was originally known, started her career on the Far Eastern routes. Her name was changed in 1904, when Messageries Maritimes bought a cargo and passenger ship that has the same name. The *Tourane* could accommodate 185 passengers in first class, 86 in second and 77 in third, until 1912, when her capacity was increased respectively to 192, 110, and 92. Like the *Indus*, the *Tourane* served in World War I, suffering the same fate as her sister ship just a fortnight later, on November 27, 1916.

241 | The port of Calcutta, c.1900. A flotilla of laden barges is shown carrying cargo out to two ships of the British India Line.

242 Left | The epitome of British apathy, an impeccably turned out couple on a P&O liner await the arrival of tea stewards, apparently oblivious to the suffocating heat.

242 Right | A P&O menu.

243 | Passengers on a British steamer en route to India and the Far East while away the time with a game of deck quoits, c. 1907.

244 | Singapore, c.1900, was a British colony at this time (it gained its independence in 1965), and the British influence is clearly visible in its architecture; passengers might have fancied themselves on the promenade of an English south coast sea resort.

245 | Brochure for the Nederland Line, the English name for the Stoomvaart Maatschappij Nederland. The Dutch company's motto *Semper Mare Navigandum* (Always sail the seas.), nicely fit the company's initials. The company was set up in Amsterdam in 1870 to operate routes between northern Europe and the Dutch East Indies, now Indonesia. Sailing from Amsterdam via Southampton and Genoa, its mail steamers would then navigate the Suez Canal and make ports of call at Java, Jakarta (then called Batavia), Surabaya and Tanjung Priok, taking on supplies of coal at Valetta, Port Said, Aden, Colombo and Sabang.

246 | Ha Long Bay, Vietnam. Long ago, according to legend, when local people were fighting off invaders from the north, the gods sent a family of dragons to help them in their struggle. They came to earth on this spot, breathing jewels and jade, which as they hit the seawater turned into islands. So seduced were the dragons by the land and its people that they decided to settle here, and Ha Long Bay, or Bay of the Descending Dragon, became home to the mother dragon. More prosaically, scientists attribute the bay's extraordinary seascape of limestone karsts to many millions of years of geological activity. A major tourist attraction, the bay was classified as a UNESCO World Heritage Site in 1994.

247 | A Messageries Maritimes poster from the 1930s featuring the romantic exoticism of Ha Long Bay, already well established as a tourist destination.

248 | The Messageries Maritimes steamer *Félix Roussel*, equipped with ten-cylinder diesel engines, operated routes to the Far East. Sumptuously decorated in Khmer-inspired style, she was renowned among passengers for her music room. Her sister ship, the *George Philippar*, sank during her return from her maiden voyage on May 16, 1932; some fifty passengers and crew lost their lives in the disaster, including the distinguished French journalist Albert Londres.

249 | The *Amiral de Kersaint* of the Chargeurs Réunis at Haiphong in 1906. At this time the city counted some 15,000 inhabitants, including a thousand or so Europeans, mostly French—hence the demand for a regular steamer service to France.

250 | Poster from the 1950s showing SS *President Wilson* of the American President Line in Shanghai.

251 Left | In the 1930s, the shipping lines vied with each other to promote their cruises. Here Messageries Maritimes tempts potential passengers with an exotic view of Hong Kong's Victoria Harbor by night.

251 Right | A Chinese junk in Victoria Harbor. The traditional local cargo and passenger vessel—fast and efficient, with its distinctive sails strengthened by horizontal battens—was a ubiquitous sight in Chinese ports.

252 | One of the docks in the port of Hong Kong around 1910. The ultra-modern quayside installations contrast with the traditional costumes still worn by the locals. The masts of service vessels can be seen in the middle distance.

253 | Moored at Ocean Terminal in Tsim Sha Tsui on the Kowloon Peninsula, Hong Kong, MS *Star Pisces*, operated by Star Cruises, the world's third largest cruise line, prepares to welcome passengers for a nighttime cruise.

254 | Equipped as it was with the latest facilities, the port of Yokohama, shown here around 1890, was able to handle the world's largest vessels. As this view shows, rails had already been laid to allow cranes to maneuver on the docks. Local people taking the air might retain traditional dress, but Yokohama was technologically as modern as the biggest ports of Europe or America.

255 | The city of Yokohama, c. 1890. On September 1, 1923 a terrible earthquake destroyed not only Yokohama but also much of Kanagawa, Shizuoka, and Tokyo, killing thousands of people.

227

3. COCK-FIGHTING.

4. A SCORE FOR BLUE.

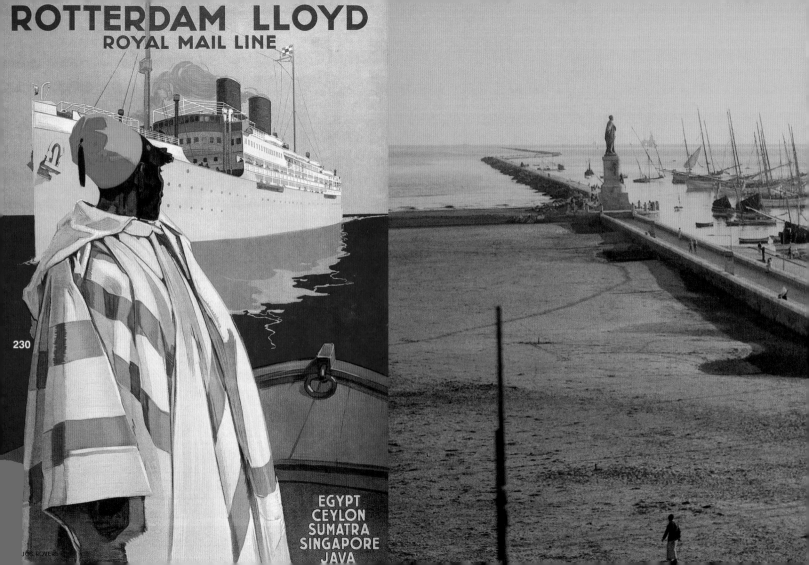

ROTTERDAM LLOYD
ROYAL MAIL LINE

230

EGYPT
CEYLON
SUMATRA
SINGAPORE
JAVA

231

GRAND HOTEL CONTINENTAL

JAMES SLAVICK SHIPCHANDLER
NAVY CONTRACTOR, P. & O. PURVEYOR &c. &c. &c.

ENGLISH STORES

GRINDLAY & Co.

233

234

237

238

239

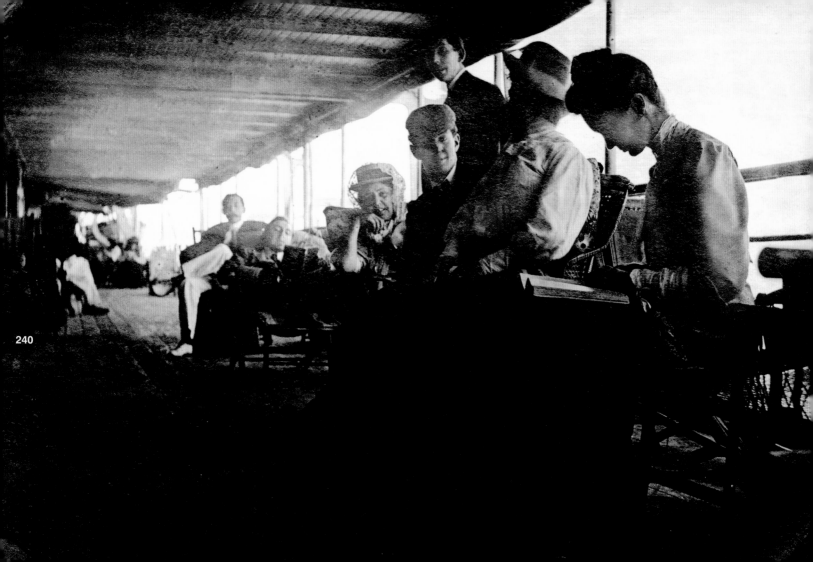

241

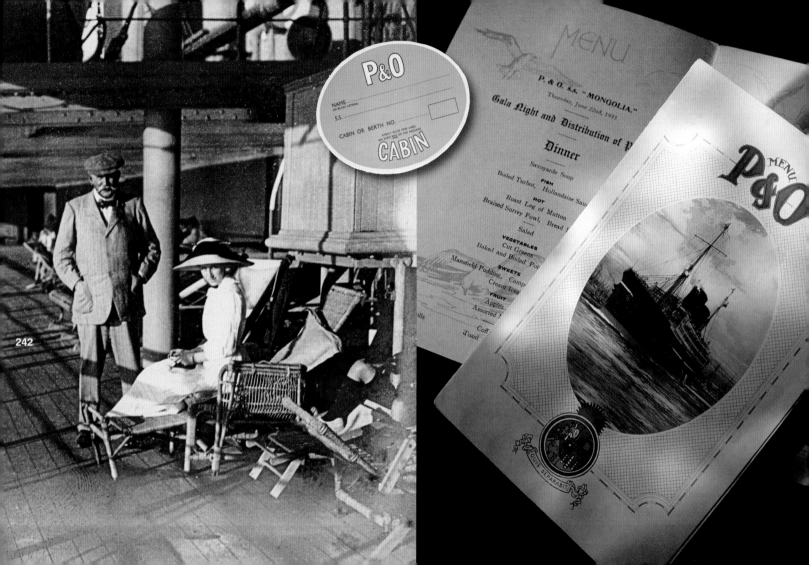

242

P&O

NAME
(IN BLOCK LETTERS)

S.S.

CABIN OR BERTH NO.

KINDLY PLACE ONE LABEL
ON EACH END OF THE PACKAGE

CABIN

MENU

P. & O. S.S. "MONGOLIA."
Thursday, June 22nd, 1933.

Gala Night and Distribution of P

Dinner

Savoyarde Soup

FISH
Boiled Turbot,   Hollandaise Sau

HOT
Roast Leg of Mutton
Braised Surrey Fowl,   Bread S

Salad

VEGETABLES
Cut Greens
Baked and Boiled Pot

SWEETS
Mansfield Pudding,   Camp
Cream Ices

FRUIT
Apples
Assorted

Coff
Toast

MENU
P&O

244

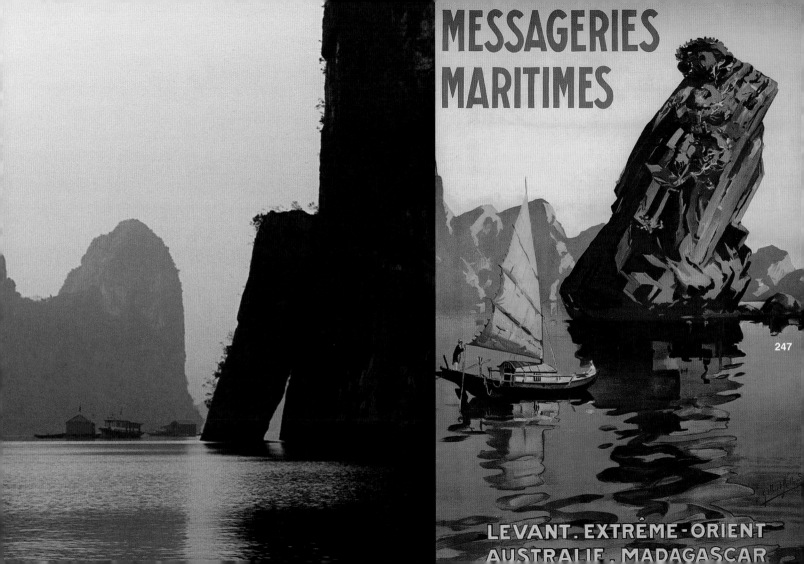

MESSAGERIES MARITIMES

247

LEVANT. EXTRÊME-ORIENT
AUSTRALIE. MADAGASCAR

248

VISITEZ
L'EXTRÊME·ORIENT
PAR LES
MESSAGERIES MARITIMES

LES IMP.ˢ FR.ˢᵉˢ RÉUNIES _ PARIS

251

254

255

THE TRANSPACIFIC CROSSING

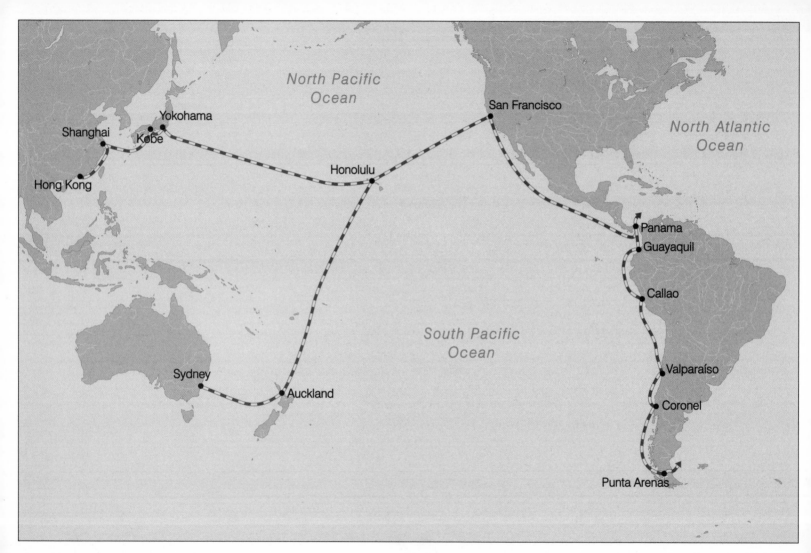

256 | Before the
construction of the
famous bridge in 1937,
Golden Gate was simply
the name of the strait
at the point where San
Francisco Bay opens
into the Pacific Ocean.

259 | The port of
Valparaiso, c.1920.

V alparaiso, Chile, toward the end of the nineteenth century was a changed city: the old men who haunted the port no longer recognized their quays, every one of which now bore the name of a shipping line, like a stamp of ownership. Behind the warehouses lining the shore, they could hear the shouts of the workers building a new town where one had barely existed a few decades earlier, a Spanish colonial-style city like so many others. Local fishermen had been squeezed out of the harbor by the great merchant ships filling it to capacity. As they took on coal, their passengers disembarked to take a tour of the town, untouched by nostalgia. As the tourists brushed past, they scarcely noticed the old men, the last surviving witnesses to the old Valparaiso that was disappearing forever. They had no conception of what it used to be like, of the change the ocean liners had brought.

Prior to the Panama Canal opening in 1914, ships out of ports on the East Coast, and from Europe, had two long and treacherous options to reach America's West Coast: either round Cape Horn via the Drake Passage or negotiate the Strait of Magellan. Before they docked at Valparaiso, the cargo-passenger ships of the Pacific Steam Navigation Company (British), the Compañía Sud-Americana de

259

Vapores (Chilean), and the Compañía Peruana de Vapores (Peruvian) would already have called at the Chilean ports of Punta Arenas and Coronel.

After Valparaiso, they would head for Callao, the main port of Peru, with its immense docks capable of handling more than 400,000 tons of cargo. As well as importing manufactured goods, Peru also exported sugar, coffee, wool, animal skins, coca leaves, crabs, and metal ores. As their ships loaded and unloaded cargo, the passengers on board were at leisure to visit nearby Lima, where they could admire the capital's modern architecture, with the first foothills of the Cordillera of the Andes rising behind. The coastline, meanwhile, was an arid desert of rock or sand for some twenty miles around Callao, without a scrap of vegetation.

The next port of call to the north, Guayaquil in Ecuador, had more charm: in the early twentieth century most of its houses were still picturesque wooden constructions. For passengers who wanted to explore farther afield, Quito lay an easy train journey away. The cruiselike voyage then continued to Panama, where passengers bound for the Far East joined ships heading for San Francisco.

In 1909, the Frenchman Gaston Pageot arrived at San Francisco from Yokohama aboard the Pacific Mail steamship *Manchuria*. His first impression of the bay was magical: he was astonished by its size ("There would be room to move for all the world's fleets here.") and by the city's skyscrapers, the first he had seen. San Francisco was also the port of entry to the United States for Chinese immigrants, who came to work in the gold and silver mines, and above all to work on the building of the first transcontinental railroad. By 1909 the flow of immigrants had slowed, but there were still plenty of passengers bound for Shanghai. Gaston Pageot complained that the two or three hundred passengers in first class were "squashed in like sardines, poorly fed, and shaken by intermittent shudders that were supremely intolerable." What conditions were like for passengers in other classes can only be imagined.

For passengers embarking at San Francisco, the Pacific crossing ended at Yokohama, the gateway to Japan that had only recently opened up to Western influence. Since the Meiji Revolution (or Restoration) of 1867, however, the country had made up for lost time, notably with British help. By 1901, the Japanese merchant fleet

261 | RMS *Oropesa* was the largest Pacific Steam Navigation Company steamer operating on the west coast of America. She offered services alternately to Cuba and Jamaica, then passed through the Panama Canal and put in at ports on the west coast of South America before returning to Liverpool via the Magellan Straits.

R M S "OROPESA"

consisted of 1,321 steamships operating principally out of the ports of Yokohama, Kobe, Osaka, Nagasaki, Hakodate, and Niigata, and the country was importing raw materials and exporting manufactured goods. When Yokohama was destroyed by the terrible earthquake of 1923, the Messageries Maritimes steamer *André Lebon* happened to be in port, and was able to take some 1,500 refugees on board. The wounded were treated by the ship's doctor and accommodated in her cabins according to the strict social etiquette then in force: Europeans in first class, Japanese notables in second, and children in third. Earthquake or not, at mealtimes each plate still sported its impeccably starched and pressed serviette, folded into a perfect cone.

Not surprisingly, the Pacific crossing was dominated by Japanese shipping lines and those on the American West Coast. The American Mail Line operated steamers from Seattle and Victoria in British Columbia, to Yokohama, Kobe, Shanghai, Hong Kong, Manila, and Honolulu. Many routes were operated in partnership with the Dollar Steamship Company. Together with the North Atlantic crossings, these were the world's most important shipping routes.

Regular connections were established from the late-nineteenth century, with three large shipping lines competing with each other. The Japanese Nippon Yusen Kaisha line (NYK) ran services to Hong Kong, China, the Hawaiian Islands, and the continental United States. Starting from Canadian ports, the Canadian Pacific Line operated the same routes and also offered a service to the

262 | Coal being loaded by manpower in the port of Nagasaki.

263 | A 1950s
advertisement for Matson
Line cruises to Hawaii.

Philippines. Both lines faced stiff competition from the
Pacific Mail Steamship Company and Dollar Line, which
also operated the same routes. What distinguished the
vessels of the different lines from each other were the level
of comfort they offered and the quality of service on board.
Mail continued to form the main cargo, and passengers
were divided into three classes: first class consisted of
wealthy tourists traveling the globe for pleasure; second
class was populated by traders and members of the
colonial service returning to their postings; and third class
was full of emigrants, mostly Chinese. The passenger
accommodation on these routes was not always filled to
capacity, but since the shipping lines were heavily
subsidized by their respective governments, they still
managed to make a profit. They continued nonetheless to
make strenuous efforts to attract passengers in all three
classes by offering services similar to those available on
the North Atlantic routes.

   Just as the opening of the Suez Canal had transformed
journeys from Europe to Africa and the East, so the
opening of the Panama Canal in 1914 brought about a
sudden revolution in shipping in American waters.
Henceforth, ships bound for Vancouver from New York

263

saved a distance of 7,875 miles over the former route via the Strait of Magellan. On the San Francisco route they saved 7,873 miles, on the Hong Kong route 5,040 miles, and if heading for Sydney, Australia 3,668 miles.

Even with the canal passage, the Pacific routes remained in the hands of the Canadians, the Americans, and the Japanese. Japanese steamers offered their passengers a decorative style that was very European, but with a touch of Japanese sophistication that proved extremely popular with a Western clientele. In 1929 and 1930, they put into service two magnificent liners, the *Asama Maru* and the *Tatsuta Maru*. In 1936, the *Tatsuta Maru* became the first merchant ship to pass under the new Bay Bridge linking San Francisco and Oakland. The Canadian Pacific line took delivery of the *Empress of Japan*, a magnificent British-built liner that was to make fifty-eight round trips between Vancouver, Yokohama, Honolulu, and Shanghai before being converted into a troop carrier during World War II.

Despite the Great Depression of 1929, the shipping lines continued to prosper in the years between the wars. In 1931, at a cost of nearly $8 million each, the Dollar Line put into service the nearly identical *President Hoover* and the *President Coolidge*. At 654 feet long and able to carry about 900 passengers, they were the two biggest passenger ships ever built in America. They were decorated in the Art Deco style, then the height of fashion, and in their advertising material claimed comparisons with the most luxurious international hotels. They had every modern luxury, including Otis elevators for convenience; swimming pools and air-conditioning for the hot days; heaters in every room for the colder nights; and many other amenities. In 1938, the Dollar family passed ownership of the liners to the US government in exchange for cancelling their outstanding debt. The liners became part of the American President Lines Ltd.; the ships continued their transpacific routes. Then, as US involvement in World War II increased in 1941, the US War Department began using the *President Coolidge* as a transport ship for reinforcing the Pacific garrisons. A month after Pearl Harbor and just ten years after launching, she was stripped of her finery, painted gunmetal gray, and mounted with guns. Once converted, she could carry 5,000 troops. The *President Coolidge* sank off the coast of Espiritu Santo, New Hebridies (now Vanuatu) in the South Pacific after striking a friendly mine in 1942. The wreck is currently open for recreational diving and many tourists once again visit the ship.

265 | SS *Korea* of the Pacific Mail sailed from San Francisco, her port of registry, to Manila via Hong Kong. When she sailed into San Francisco for the first time, in August 1902, she was the largest vessel ever to have entered harbor there.

cinemas, and restaurants proposing a variety of menus: little short of a dream.

At this time, European lines continued to take the eastern route to the Far East, secure in the knowledge that there were numerous ports of call where they could embark and disembark passengers and cargo. In the 1950s, P&O launched a regular round-the-world service, extending its Indian route via Fremantle, Melbourne, and Sydney, Australia; Auckland, New Zealand; Honolulu, Hawaii; Vancouver, British Columbia; San Francisco and Los Angeles; Acapulco, Mexico; the Panama Canal; Nassau, Bahamas; Port Everglades, Florida; Bermuda; Lisbon, Portugal; and Le Havre, France. Plying this itinerary, on voyages that were alternately eastbound and westbound, were the magnificent liners *Oriana* and *Arcadia*, offering two classes of accommodations.

On August 21, 1959, Hawaii became the fiftieth state of the Union, an act that lent official recognition to the archipelago's strategic importance to the United States, which continues to this day. With its breathtaking natural beauty and charismatic culture, not to mention Honolulu's reputation as a surfers' paradise, Hawaii was destined to become a major tourist destination, and with hundreds of

In the immediate aftermath of the war, a new generation of American cruise passenger made their appearance; they were young (generally under forty) and in search of novelty. It was for this clientele that in 1947 American President Lines launched its new liners, the *President Cleveland* and the *President Wilson*, with air-conditioned cabins, a swimming pool for each class, shops,

266 | Waving goodbye on wharf 91B at Pyrmont Bay, Sydney, in the 1940s.

267 | A Matson Line luggage label.

islands making up the volcanic chain, it is perfect for cruising.

With the advent of the Boeing 747 jumbo jet in 1970, the transpacific route was no longer viable for passenger traffic. But the beaches of the Pacific promised idyllic scenery and halcyon peace, and so cruise liners quickly stepped into the breach. While Mediterranean cruises offer cultural tourism, Pacific cruises offer total relaxation, sport, and more recently, green tourism.

An emblem of the change that had taken place in a century of ocean liners—from transporting cargo and immigrants along with first-class passengers to being purely pleasure crafts—came in the form of the *Pacific Princess*, owned and operated by Princess Cruises. From 1977 to 1987, this ship gained celebrity on *The Love Boat*, a heady mixture of glamour and adventure with an ever-changing cast of characters in search of romance.

The *Makura* steamed through the islands of the Fiji group, and we stopped twenty-two hours at the capital, Suva, where cabs and taxis were obtained for hire, "to see the sights." A cricket match was played between a Suva club and an eleven selected from our passengers. The match resulted in a score of 128 to 28 in favor of the local team.

At Suva and Honolulu the natives swim around the steamer, diving for the silver coins thrown overboard by passengers. It is rare sport.

FRANK COFFEE,
Forty Years on the Pacific,
November 1913

267

Sept. 3. In 9° 50' north latitude, at breakfast. Approaching the equator on a long slant. Those of us who have never seen the equator are a good deal excited. I think I would rather see it than any other thing in the world. We entered the "doldrums" last night—variable winds, bursts of rain, intervals of calm, with chopping seas and a wobbly and drunken motion to the ship— a condition of things findable in other regions sometimes, but present in the doldrums always. The globe-girdling belt called the doldrums is 20 degrees wide, and the thread called the equator lies along the middle of it. . . .

Sept. 5. Closing in on the equator this noon. A sailor explained to a young girl that the ship's speed is poor because we are climbing up the bulge toward the center of the globe; but that when we should once get over, at the equator, and start down-hill, we should fly. When she asked him the other day what the foreyard was, he said it was the front yard, the open area in the front end of the ship. That man has a good deal of learning stored up, and the girl is likely to get it all.

Afternoon. Crossed the equator. In the distance it looked like a blue ribbon stretched across the ocean. Several passengers kodak'd it. We had no fool ceremonies, no fantastics, no horse-play. All that sort of thing has gone out. In old times a sailor, dressed as Neptune, used to come in over the bows, with his suite, and lather up and shave everybody who was crossing the equator for the first time, and then cleanse these unfortunates by swinging them from the yardarm and ducking them three times in the sea. This was considered funny. Nobody knows why. No, that is not true. We do know why. Such a thing could never be funny on land; no part of the old-time grotesque performances gotten up on shipboard to celebrate the passage of the line could ever be funny on shore—they would seem dreary and witless to shore people. But the shore people would change their minds about it at sea, on a long voyage. On such a voyage, with its eternal monotonies, people's intellects deteriorate; the owners of the intellects soon reach a point where they almost seem to prefer childish things to things of a maturer degree. One is often surprised at the juvenilities which grown people indulge in at sea, and the interest they take in them, and the consuming enjoyment they get out of them. This is on long voyages only. The mind gradually becomes inert, dull, blunted; it loses its accustomed interest in intellectual things; nothing but horseplay can rouse it, nothing but wild and foolish grotesqueries can entertain it. On short voyages it makes no such exposure of itself; it hasn't time to slump down to this sorrowful level.

269

MARK TWAIN, *Following the Equator,* 1897

Yesterday morning at 6:30 I was aroused by the news that "The Islands" were in sight. Oahu in the distance, a group of grey, barren peaks rising verdureless out of the lonely sea . . . As we approached, the island changed its character. There were lofty peaks, truly—grey and red, sun-scorched, and wind-bleached, glowing here and there with traces of their fiery origin; but they were cleft by deep chasms and ravines of cool shade and entrancing greenness, and falling water streaked their sides—a most welcome vision after eleven months of the desert sea, and the dusty browns of Australia and New Zealand. . . . The surf ran white and pure over the environing coral reef, and is we passed through the narrow channel, we almost saw the coral forests deep down under the Nevada's keel; the coral fishers plied their graceful trade; canoes with outriggers rode the combers, and glided with inconceivable rapidity round out ship; amphibious brown beings sported in the transparent waves; and within the reef lay a calm surface of water of a wonderful blue, entered by a narrow, intricate passage of the deepest indigo. And beyond the reef and beyond the blue, nestling among cocoanut trees and bananas, umbrella trees and breadfruits, oranges, mangoes, hibiscus, algaroba, and passion-flowers, almost hidden in the deep, dense greenery, was Honolulu. Bright blossom of a summer sea! Fair Paradise of the Pacific

ISABELLA BIRD, Hawaiian Hotel, Honolulu, January 26, 1875

273 | The *Sonoma* of the Matson Line in San Francisco, 1926. Built in Philadelphia for the Oceanic Steamship Company, this magnificent liner sailed between the United States and Australia. After a long and uneventful career, she was broken up in 1934.

274 | As they left San Francisco Bay, ships sailed past the ferry terminal.

275 | An officer on the SS *Vermont* enjoys a photo opportunity with four charming lady passengers, c. 1905. The *Vermont* sailed the west coast of America to Chile.

276–77 | The entrance to the Panama Canal viewed from the Pacific Ocean. The progress of this colossal feat of engineering, accomplished by John Frank Stevens and George Washington Goethals in 1914 (after a failed attempt by the French under Ferdinand de Lesseps in the 1880s, which had to be abandoned after the loss of more than 20,000 lives) was followed by the American public with almost overwhelming enthusiasm.
Over two years before its opening, prompted by a rumor that navigation would be attempted in 1913, hundreds of tourists booked places on steamers, obliging the shipping lines to take unprecedented measures. The *New York Times* of February 14, 1912 reported that officers' cabins were hired by passengers with no apparent concern for either price or levels of comfort, as long as they could see the tremendous engineering works before they were flooded with water.

278 | Advertisement for the Panama Mail Steamship Company. In 1927, this line operated five luxury liners between San Francisco and New York via the Panama Canal: the *Colombia, Ecuador, Venezuela, City of San Francisco,* and *City of Panama.* The ships put in at Los Angeles and a number of ports in Mexico, Guatemala, El Salvador, Honduras, Nicaragua, Costa Rica, and Colombia.

279 | A steamer negotiating a lock on the Panama Canal. Entering the canal from the Pacific, ships first encounter the two-stage Miraflores lock system, followed by the Pedro Miguel lock. Together these raise vessels to the level of Lake Gatún, where a three-stage flight of locks drops them back to sea level. The Gatún locks are filled using water from the artificial lake—approximately 52 million gallons (197 million liters) of water with each operation. Each of the lock systems operates in both directions simultaneously, in principal allowing ships to pass each other. However large ships cannot safely pass in both directions in the Gaillard cut, so often the locks are used in the same direction for a time before allowing ships to pass in the other direction.

280 | Photographs taken by a passenger on the Dutch liner *Ryndam* as she navigated the Panama Canal in the 1920s, showing installations and facilities along the canal and a cargo ship negotiating an adjacent lock. SS *Ryndam* was built by Harland & Wolff in Belfast for the Holland America Line in 1901. As well as a regular service across the North Atlantic, she also provided numerous cruises of the Pacific.

281 | A steamer enters one of the Gatún locks at a stately pace guided by a locomotive mule seen abreast of the ship and to the left. Railway lines on the opposite bank will enable other mules to work in tandem as the ship approaches the lock chamber.

282 | The liner *Empress of Scotland* of the Canadian Pacific Railway Company navigating the Gaillard Cut in the Panama Canal in the 1930s. To the right, a small tourist plane flies in low to admire the spectacle. At this point the canal at its original 300 feet (91.5 meters) was too narrow for two ships to pass. In the 1960s the cut would be expanded to 500 feet (152.4 meters) and it is currently undergoing expansion to 630 feet (192 meters) to accommodate large ships moving in both directions.

283 Top | A Pacific Panama Line postcard showing one of its steamers negotiating the Pedro Miguel lock.

283 Right | Navigating the length of the Panama Canal took about twelve hours, with the successive locks and mules providing a spectacle of endless fascination for passengers.

284 | On the interminable voyage from San Francisco to Honolulu and Yokohama, crews vied with each other to think up distractions for passengers. This photograph shows a round of a game called Are you there, Bill?, an alarming-looking variant on blindman's buff involving two blindfolded passengers flailing at each other with rubber truncheons (wrapped in cloth to soften the blows), to the evident amusement of onlookers.

285 | On the way out to the warm waters of Honolulu, cruise ships sailed through cooler waters. Cosily wrapped up in a coat with a fur collar, this young woman absorbed in her book is the only passenger to brave the chill of the promenade deck.

286 | Resplendent in their costumes for the fancy dress ball that traditionally celebrated the end of the long Pacific crossing, passengers pose for a group photograph. Only the captain, seated at the extreme right, and the officer standing behind him preserve their dignity intact.

287 | On her arrival in Honolulu around 1930, a Matson Line cruise ship is greeted by a flotilla of small motorboats and traditional Hawaiian dugout canoes.

288–89 | Souvenirs collected by a passenger on the *President Hayes* of the Dollar Steamship Line in March 1932, including the menu for a Rabelaisian goodbye dinner for passengers leaving the ship at Honolulu, and photographs of Hawaii.

290–91 | An album of happy memories of a cruise on the Matson Line steamer *Matsonia* in October 1939.

292 Left | Passengers on the Dutch ship *Ryndam* gamely play the ukulele on the approach to Honolulu in 1927. While the lei, or flower garlands, were a traditional form of greeting visitors, the ukulele was a more recent introduction. Brought to Hawaii in 1879 by some Portuguese cabinetmakers, it was immediately adopted by the islanders, and today is integral to traditional Hawaiian music.

292 Right | Advertisement for the Matson Line in 1953.

293 | The Matson Line cruise ship *Lurline* leaving port at San Francisco for her first post-war outing on April 15, 1948. As tradition demanded, passengers on board shower friends and family left behind on terra firma with a blizzard of tickertape.

294–95 | The *Heiyo Maru* of the Nippon Yusen Kaisha Line (NYK) in Victoria Harbor, Hong Kong. Launched in 1930, this vessel served routes to the west coast of America and Hawaii. Converted into a troop carrier during

World War II, she was torpedoed and sunk by the American submarine USS *Whale* on January 17, 1943.

296 | The Canadian Pacific liner *Empress of Russia* sailing down Tokyo Bay after leaving Yokohama en route for Vancouver. Inset: Japanese line Nippon Yusen Kaisha (NYK) badge.

297 | A stateroom on the *Asama Maru*, c.1908. The skilful blending of European and Japanese decorative styles proved irresistible to western passengers.

298 | William H. Taft, Secretary of War and future President, leaves the port of Yokohama in July 1905. Behind his portly figure is Miss Alice Roosevelt, daughter of President Roosevelt, who accompanied Taft on his Far Eastern tour and who observed on her return to America that this had been "the most pleasant, the most interesting, and the most instructive trip I have ever taken." A reception committee of Japanese dignitaries is also present to greet distinguished visitors arriving on the *Manchuria*, of the Pacific Mail Steamship Company.

299 | Doubtless they spent the rest of the voyage from San Francisco in more nondescript attire, but for their arrival in

Japan—where they will transfer to a ferry for the rest of the journey home— these Korean passengers are magnificent in their national dress.

300 | The port of Auckland, New Zealand, toward the end of the nineteenth century. At this time, only Queen Street Wharf could accommodate ocean liners—and then only of low tonnage—alongside cargo and passenger ships. Not until the 1930s did improvements to the docks' infrastructure make it possible for great cruise ships from London, Sydney, and San Francisco to berth here.

301 | The *Australia* (1875–1905), of the Pacific Mail Steamship Company, preparing to set sail from Sydney, c.1900.

302–3 | The Cunard superliner *Queen Mary 2* making her majestic entrance into Sydney harbor. From April to November she offers a regular transatlantic service between Europe and North America; during the rest of the year she cruises to the Mediterranean, the Caribbean, and Scandinavia. In January every year she sets off on a world cruise lasting 101 nights.

SOHOMA

273

PANAMA MAIL
STEAMSHIP COMPANY

AIRVIEW OF THE
PANAMA CANAL ZONE

PANAMA MAIL
S.S. CO.

SAN FRANCISCO-
NEW YORK
SERVICE
Thru The
PANAMA
CANAL

"THE
CRUISE
THAT
SOOTHES
AND
RESTS
AND
DELIGHTS"

ATLANTIC OCEAN

COLON
CRISTOBAL

RIO CHAGRES

GATUN LOCKS   ELEVA. 85'

GATUN DAM

GATUN LAKE

PANAMA R.R.

RIO CHAGRES

CANAL ZONE

GAILLARD CUT

OLD PANAMA

CANAL ZONE

PEDRO MIGUEL LOCKS   ELEVA. 85'
MIRAFLORES LOCKS

ANCON   PANAMA
BALBOA

PACIFIC OCEAN

GUATEMALA

99007704

286

287

Matson Lines

HONOLULU

★

STATEROOM

GUEST LIST

288

DOLLAR STEAMSHIP LINES

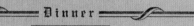

Pleasanton Hotel
HONOLULU, T. H.

DINNER D'ADIEU TO OUR HONOLULU PASSENGERS
S. S. "PRESIDENT HAYES"
O. A. Pierson, Commander.

— Dinner —

Hors D' Oeuvres

Fresh Lobster Cocktail

Croutons au Chutney   Cheese Straws   Calif. Ripe Olives

Stuffed Celery en Branche   Chow Chow

SOUP

Poulet a la Reine   Cold Consomme

FISH

Boiled Fresh Chicken Halibut, Oyster Sauce

ENTREES

Petit Entrecote Steak, Fresh Mushroom Sauce

Calves Sweetbread Patties

Peach a la Conde

ROASTS

Young Vermont Turkey with Sage Dressing & Cranberry Sauce

VEGETABLES

Buttered Summer Squash   Boiled Rice   String Beans au Beurre

POTATOES:---   Boiled   Browned

COLD BUFFET

Prime Ribs of Beef   Salami Sausage   York Ham

SALAD

Waldorf   Lettuce

DESSERT & PASTRY

Fig Pudding, Sweet Sauce

Green Apple Pie   Petit Fours

Special Frozen Pudding & Wafers

CHEESE

American   Roquefort   Swiss

Toasted Crackers   Chilled Fresh Fruits

Asst. Nuts   Layer Raisins

Golden Dates   A. D. Mints

— Demi Tasse —

Thomas Cope, Chief Steward   Thursday March 24sh. 1932

ALOHA OE

Aloha Tower and Harbor, Honolulu

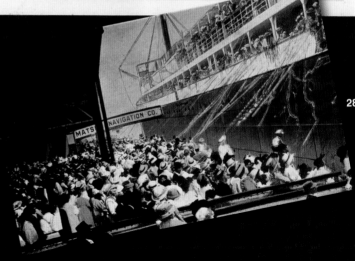

MATSON NAVIGATION CO.

28

MATSON NAVIGATION COMPANY THE OCEANIC STEAMSHIP COMPANY

SERIAL NUMBER **29771**

IDENTIFICATION CHECK

FORM NUMBER TS-21

ONE WAY CABIN CLASS CONTRACT TICKET

TO **HONOLULU**

FROM **LOS ANGELES HARBOR**

THIS IDENTIFICATION CHECK IS TO BE RETAINED BY PASSENGER UNTIL COMPLETION OF VOYAGE

NAMES OF PASSENGERS IN FULL

MINSON, MRS. R. W.
X X X X X X X
REMARKS

NOTICE—NOT GOOD FOR PASSAGE UNTIL RESERVATION FOR A SPECIFIED SAILING HAS BEEN SECURED.

$85.00

GROSS VALUE OF TICKET

PASSENGERS FROM HONOLULU
...THE JOURNEY FROM ...OWN ABOVE, IS AVAIL- ...CALIFORNIA PORT ONLY. ...ERE THE PURSER WILL. ...CHANGE ROOM. ASSIGN ...COMMODATION BEYOND.

RESERVATIONS

CARRIER **MATSON NAVIGATION COMPANY** TO **HONOLULU**
FROM **LOS ANGELES HARBOR** DATE **OCT. 5, 1939** HOUR **12**
S.S. **MATSONIA** VOY. **43**
ROOM **369**
BERTH **B**

FORM
AGENT **C. J. JONES STEAMSHIP AGENCY**
STREET **383 E. COLORADO STREET**
CITY **PASADENA, CALIFORNIA**

NO.   ORDER HONORED   VALUE

IDENTIFICATION CHECK
(TO BE RETAINED DURING THE VOYAGE
(NOT GOOD FOR PASSAGE)

PRINTED IN U.S.A.

Honolulu, I'm Coming Back Again
[CHORUS]

"I seem to hear the Pali calling me,
I seem to hear the surf at Waikiki,
And from Pacific Heights,
I seem to see the lights,
Of a city that is very dear to me.
I seem to see the waving sugar cane;
The coco palms, all nodding in the rain;
In fancy I am led
Back to dear old Diamond Head—
Honolulu, I'm coming back again!"

OCEANIC LINE
...R...
...ET...
ZEALAND · AUSTRALIA

292

Glad to Have You Aboard

There are no strangers on the LURLINE. Captain Johnson makes you feel right at home with his cordial "*Aloha*" ...his "Welcome Aboard!" And all around you is the spirit of Hawaii. It invites you to all kinds of fun and relaxation ... seagoing sports, parties, movies, dancing. It adds zest to your enjoyment of matchless food and of well-serviced, luxurious living. Only Matson know-how, product of nearly three-quarters of a century on the Pacific, could weave the gaiety and color of Hawaii so intimately into your voyage on the LURLINE. What a vacation ... all included in your round-trip fare!

See your Travel Agent or any Matson Lines office: New York, Chicago, San Francisco, Seattle, Portland, Los Angeles, San Diego, Honolulu. And book round trip on the LURLINE!

The Lurline is Hawaii

Matson Lines

For the finest travel, the LURLINE... for the finest freight service, the Matson cargo fleet...to and from Hawaii.

THE LURLINE SAILS FROM SAN FRANCISCO AND LOS ANGELES ALTERNATELY

294

296

298

SARGOOD, SON & EWEN, WAREHOUSEMEN.

THE AUCKLAND
PAPER BAG PRINTING WORKS

ATKIN CARRIAGE FACTORY

ATKIN BROS.

301

ROUTES OF ICE AND GOLD

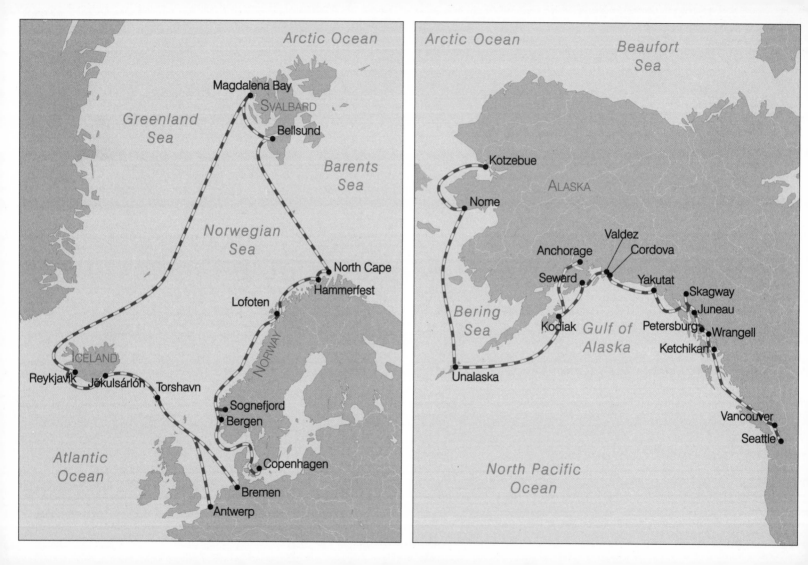

304 | Passengers board small boats to go ashore to visit Magdalena Fjord in Spitzbergen, c.1930.

307 | Landing stage of the Alaska Steamship Company in Seattle.

In the summer of 1896, four men were on a fishing expedition in the Klondike. Robert Henderson, a gold prospector, had been the first to spot "the colors" in a nearby creek, but it was his companions, George Carmack and the Tagish Indians Skookum Jim Mason and Tagish Charlie, who were to make a startling discovery in a tributary of the Yukon River in Canada, near its confluence with the Klondike. There had always been gold in these parts, but in derisory amounts; on August 16, all that changed. Which of the three men bending over the waters of Rabbit Creek saw it first is still disputed, though it was believed to be Skookum Jim Mason. What he spotted was a gold nugget the size of a dime. Between them, they had just discovered the richest gold deposits in Canada.

The discovery was to be the signal for the biggest gold rush in history. While rumors of the gold had been slowly spreading, it wasn't until July 17, 1897, when the *Excelsior* steamed into San Francisco harbor with more than $500,000 in Klondike gold that the true craze began. The passengers on board might have looked like tramps, but the gold had made them rich beyond their wildest dreams. When the *Portland* arrived in Seattle three days later it was the same story: stowed in the luggage of the ragged

collection of men and a few women who disembarked was a small fortune.

The news traveled fast: you only had to bend down and there it was; all you had to do was pick it up! But getting to this new El Dorado required determination and stamina. On July 18, the offices of the Alaska Commercial Company were overrun with "stampeders" and had sold out all slots on the *Excelsior* for the return trip, turning away ten times the number of passengers the ship could carry. Prospectors rushed to the Klondike in the thousands and the going rate for passage soon reached $1,000, causing a kind of gold rush for the shipping companies,

and ships of every kind were pressed into service to transport the men north, often squeezing more than five-times the number of passengers the ships were meant to carry. Taking an expensive, overcrowded ship was still better than the alternative overland route, which involved scaling steep and treacherous mountain passes, crossing glaciers, and opening up paths through a hostile wilderness. Many died on the way, many more gave up, exhausted; only months later would the most tenacious arrive at their destination.

By sea and river the journey was scarcely less grueling. Steamers—mostly with side paddles—departed from San Francisco, called at Seattle and Vancouver, then headed northwest to round the Alaskan Peninsula and reach the mouth of the Yukon. Then they navigated the river upstream as far as the Klondike, where the prospectors disembarked. In winter the river would freeze and they would have to complete the journey on foot, without even the scant level of comfort offered by the steamers.

On board the cabins were packed, and the food served in what was ambitiously called the dining room was as disgusting as it was inadequate. The dining room on the coal-carrier-turned-passenger-ship the *Willamette*, had

308 | SS *Alameda* was built in Philadelphia in 1883 for the Oceanic Steamship Company. Bought in 1910 by the Alaska Steamship Company, she was used to transport railroad construction materials from Seattle to Anchorage. In 1921 she struck a reef off Seward; there were no casualties, and the *Alameda* was repaired and put back into service. Later that same year she caught fire while in dock at Seattle. She was broken up in 1935.

309 | SS *Dorothy Alexander* of the Pacific Steamship Company in the harbor at Sitka, c.1930.

309

been designed to accommodate a mere sixty-five diners, but the owners had jammed more than 800 passengers and 300 animals on the vessel, all without sweeping up any of the coal dust. All this might have been easier to ignore had the boats been in seaworthy condition, which was far from the case. So frantic was the demand that some operators simply brought back into service vessels that would normally have been scrapped. To add to the adventure, many of the ships' captains were unfamiliar with the coast of Alaska and the dangers for shipping in the region. Accidents were commonplace.

But the gold diggers were not easily discouraged, paying the inflated prices for their passage, to the point where the sea route to the Klondike became known as the rich man's route. By 1898 most of the good land claims had been made and the gold became more difficult to access. Prospecting had become an industry, and there was no room left for small-scale panners. Now it seemed that new deposits discovered in Nome, Alaska offered more riches, so off they set in a new direction.

Whether or not they struck it lucky, many of the stampeders did not remain unmoved by the wild beauty of the Alaskan landscape, and especially its rugged coastline.

310 | These three Tingit girls in regional dress have boarded a liner at Yakutat in order to sell local crafts.

311 | Tourists from a passenger liner admire Child's Glacier, about 50 miles (80 kilometers) from Cordova, Alaska, c.1920.

A few of the shrewder among them quickly abandoned their gold prospecting in order to organize cruises in Alaska. In 1898, the English gentleman Harry de Windt, who dubbed southern Alaska "the Norway of America," published a book of his journey made two-years prior, *Through the Gold-Fields of Alaska to Bering Straits*. De Windt wrote:

310

Juneau, today, is thronged with gaily dressed tourists disgorged by the steamer that has brought us from Victoria: a two-days' journey through fjords of indescribable beauty, past towering peaks of granite, densely wooded valleys, and glaciers of clear blue crystal washed by the waves of the sea.

Tourist cruises soon developed into an industry. The Alaska Steamship Company, founded in 1895, before the Klondike gold rush, and based in Seattle, was a major player. By the eve of World War II it had grown to operate eighteen steamers, of which the *Alaska, Aleutian, Yukon, Mount McKinley, Victoria,* and *Baranof* were dedicated to the tourist routes from Seattle. After traveling the Inside Passage, a sheltered coastal route between the mainland and coastal islands of Canada and the Alaskan Panhandle, liners would go onto various ports such as Ketchikan, salmon capital of the world; followed by ports of call at Wrangell, with its famous totem pole; Sitka, site of the flag-raising ceremony to mark America's purchase of Alaska from Russia in 1867; Juneau, the capital since 1906; Haines, for many years the northernmost outpost of the United States Army; Petersburg, famous for its fisheries; the gold rush town of Skagway; the copper-ore mining settlement of Cordova; Valdez and the massive Columbia Glacier; and

finally Seward, the terminus for scheduled steamers. Tourist cruises, however, would go on to the villages of Seldovia and Kodiak. Some lines even offered passages through the Bering Strait to Kotzebue, facing Siberia in the Arctic Circle.

Other ice routes were also worth gold, and not just because of the tourist trade. In the late nineteenth century, Norway had few roads: a letter posted in Trondheim would take three weeks to reach Hammerfest in summer, and as long as five months in winter. In 1891, the Norwegian authorities once again raised the old idea of establishing a sea link, but the shipping lines objected that navigation was too perilous in Norwegian waters, especially in winter. The challenge was finally taken up by Richard With, a merchant sea captain who founded the Vesteraalens Dampskibsselskap coastal steamer company in 1881. In May 1893, With signed a contract with the Norwegian government under which he undertook to provide a weekly service between Trondheim and Hammerfest, with ports of call at Rørvik, Brønnøysund, Sandnessjøen, Bodø, Svolvær, Lødingen, Harstad, Tromsø, and Skjervøy. On July 2, the steamer *Vesterålen* inaugurated the route, called the Hurtigruten, or coastal express. It completed the first trip from Trondheim to Hammerfast in just sixty-seven hours; the route was an instant success.

For many settlements, the coastal express offered a vital lifeline, a quick and comfortable means of getting up and down the coast. In the last years of the nineteenth century, the route was extended to Vadsø in the north and to Bergen and later Stavanger in the south and now covers almost the entire length of the country.

The early twentieth century saw mass emigration from the Scandinavian countries to America. The Det Nordenfjeldske Dampskibsselskab, which already operated a route from Trondheim to Bergen and Stavanger, extended its route to Newcastle. In 1910, the Norwegian America Line took advantage of the flood of emigrants by opening a route between Oslo and New York, operated by the liners *Kristianiafjord, Bergensfjord, Oslofjord*, and *Stavangerfjord*. These routes, however, were not to survive the advent of commercial jet travel.

The coastal express, meanwhile, retains a healthy trade, even though it carries much less freight than in the past. But passenger traffic on the Hurtigruten line continues strongly, on what is indisputably the world's most beautiful sea route. From the late nineteenth century, German lines such as the Hapag and Norddeutscher Lloyd offered "polar cruises," which proved increasingly popular with tourists. Some of these cruises started from Edinburgh, skirted Iceland via the Faroe Islands off Denmark, to reach the snowy peaks and glaciers of Spitsbergen in the Svalbard archipelago, and finally North Cape (Nordkapp), Norway, where the Atlantic Ocean meets the Arctic Ocean.

Until a road was constructed in 1956, the most intrepid passengers would toil up the one thousand and eight steps leading from Hornvika to the top of the cliff at Nordkapp, a dizzying 1,007 feet (307 meters). The grueling hour-and-a-

314 | A Sami family in front of their tents.

315 | The crew of SS *Bremen* celebrate crossing the Arctic Circle, 1928.

314

Polar
Stimmung
1928

§ 11

BERLIN
BREMEN

315

half-climb was amply rewarded by the breathtaking view, especially during the months of the midnight sun, from mid-May to late July. On their return to the ship, passengers would be rewarded with mulled wine and a certificate to keep.

These cruises would then continue along the Hurtigruten, visiting picturesque villages, majestic fjords, and imposing glaciers including Hammerfest, Lyngseidet, Tromsø, Merok, Gudvangen, and Odda. A highlight was a visit to a Sami community. In the summer of 1935, the chef of the SS *Albertville* of the Compagnie Maritime de Belgique marked her port call at Lyngseidet, on the line's twenty-third cruise to North Cape and the Norwegian fjords, with a special menu. Starters included brawn of seal meat, seagull *à l'escavêche*, and cod liver pâté; the *pièces de résistance* were wolf seal *gratiné*, whalemeat, haunch of polar bear, reindeer *en daube*, and penguin flipper with polar rice; and the feast was rounded off with pickled herrings.

Although the route remained a scheduled service, it became so popular with tourists that operators on the Hurtigruten were obliged to adapt vessels to suit the needs of the new clientele. What were once simple ferries now

316 | The Hapag liner SS *Blücher* in Geiranger Fjord, c.1910.

rival the latest cruise liners in comfort and luxury, with spacious cabins, luxury suites, swimming pools and—this being Scandinavia—saunas. The latest generation of cruise ships—*Kong Harald* and *Richard With* of 1993, *Nordlys* of 1994, *Nordkapp* and *Polarlys* of 1996, *NordNorge* of 1997, *Finnmarken* and *Trollfjord* of 2002, and *Midnatsol* of 2003— are all equipped with panoramic lounges on their top deck, so that passengers can admire the breathtaking spectacle of the fjords regardless of the weather.

The *Fram* of 2007, meanwhile, spends summer in the

Northern Hemisphere, navigating the coast of Greenland to the limits of the ice field, before heading south for the Southern Hemisphere summer, which she spends taking passengers from Ushuaia in Argentina to the Antarctic. Those fortunate enough to sail aboard her in both hemispheres are thus able to compare the ice sheet of the Arctic, formed from frozen seawater, with the icebergs of Antarctica, formed from freshwater glaciers. Passengers on these ecological cruises cannot fail to be impressed by the urgency of preserving these spectacular natural wildernesses.

Today, the northeast and northwest passages, which polar explorers have dreamed of for so long, are becoming a reality. If climate change continues at the present rate, shipping routes will soon be possible between Europe and the Pacific Ocean via the northern coast of Siberia. If the polar ice sheet continues to melt, ships will be able to navigate from the Atlantic to the Pacific between the islands of the Canadian Arctic—a scenario worthy of Jules Verne in *The Purchase of the North Pole*. But, however stirring the idea of the northeast and northwest passages may be, we must hope the day never comes when these fabled routes become navigable by ship.

While excessive heat is met with in many parts during the summer the thermometer ranged from 50° to 60° during the Alaska trip in August, 1916. And there is no danger of becoming seasick in these waters, as there is hardly a ripple except that caused by the steamer. A fellow passenger, a silk manufacturer, pointed out to me during this trip that it was from the steamer's wake that the first idea of designing watered silk was obtained.

FRANK COFFEE,
aboard the *Princess Sophia*, 1916

Keeping far out, to avoid certain sunken rocks, till we had come opposite South Gat, we ran for Magdalena Bay. Its fame is indeed well deserved. The snow-fairies possess few lovelier retreats in all the glacier regions of the world. There was no time to spare, for the swift south gale was bringing up a storm of snow which came with the enveloping clouds, and was about to overflow the hills into the bay. The heaving sea, the dashing water, the tumbling boat, the noisy wind, the low-racing clouds, tearing down over the hills like some tidal wave breaking on a rock-bound coast, formed a combination of circumstances which gave to the view of Magdalena Bay a setting of excitement. There was a vision of purest glaciers, tumbling between jagged and jutting ridges of aiguilles, seamed by steep couloirs, a vision of glaciers with wide blue-fronted snouts washed by the blue sea, a radiating series of ice-rivers and cataracts stretching back on all sides into the icy interior. The buttress arêtes were like so many Peteret ridges, powdered with fresh snow on such little ledges as would retain it. A moment only we beheld these things; the curtain descended, and they were gone.

SIR WILLIAM MARTIN CONWAY, *The First Crossing of Spitsbergen*, 1897

321 | Like many other shipping lines, the Hamburg-Amerika Linie produced sumptuous publicity brochures as gifts for its wealthy passengers. This leather-bound album from around 1910 contains photographs of a cruise from Edinburgh to Iceland, Spitzbergen, North Cape, the Norwegian fjords, and Copenhagen.

322 | Ice floes in Jökulsárlón Bay, Iceland. While icebergs—massive chunks of ice broken off from glaciers—are frozen freshwater, pack ice such as this is the frozen crust of seawater.

323 | Weaving a path between drift ice from Kongsfjorden (Kings Bay) in Svalbard, Spitzbergen, this liner of the Hamburg-Südamerikanische line offers her passengers a majestic spectacle, c.1930.

324 | As a launch ferries passengers from the Hapag steamer *Blücher* ashore somewhere in Spitzbergen around 1910, two lady passengers proffer their tickets for this optional excursion to a local official. The *Blücher* could accommodate 390 passengers in first class, 230 in second and 1550 in third. During the World War I she

remained out of commission at Pernambuco in Brazil until June 1, 1917, when she was seized by the Brazilian authorities and renamed *Leopoldina*. Subsequently she was handed over to the Compagnie Générale Transatlantique, which refitted her and launched her on the Le Havre–New York route as the *Suffren*. She was scrapped in 1929.

325 | On Advent Bay in Spitzbergen, Norway, the local authorities built this little timber lodge, shown in this photochrom, c.1900, to welcome tourists and direct them to the launches that would ferry them back to their cruise ships. Arriving passengers, meanwhile, would meet up here before setting off on excursions.

326–27 | Pages from a souvenir album kept by a passenger on the Belgian cruise liner *Albertville* of the Compagnie Maritime Belge line. Organized by the Bennett travel agency, the cruise visited North Cape and the fjords of Norway, August 10–30, 1935.

328 | Lying at a latitude of 70° 39' 48"N, Hammerfest in Norway can claim to be the northernmost city in Europe. The granite Meridian Column, topped

by a globe, was erected in 1854 to commemorate the first international measurement of the earth's circumference. In 2005 it was added to UNESCO's World Heritage List.

329 | The midnight sun over North Cape, c.1900.

330 | Raftsund viewed from Digermulen in the Lofoten Islands. The glorious natural beauties of these unspoiled islands, with their steep rocky coasts and peaks, lush grasslands, little fishing harbors and warm summer temperatures, rapidly made the Lofoten archipelago a popular tourist destination. Photochrom, c.1900.

331 | Advertising brochure for Hapag cruises to Norway in 1932. The proximity of Germany to Norway made it an accessible for German shipping lines to be the first to offer cruises to the far north in the late nineteenth century.

332 | An ice cave in the Supphellebreen Glacier in Sognefjord, c.1900. This glacier has now divided in two, with the lower section in the valley doomed to melt and vanish.

333 | Two female passengers from a cruise liner pose for a photograph in front of the end moraine of the Kjendalsbreen Glacier at Loen, c.1910. Tourism in the Polar Regions was still a novelty at this period, reserved even more than other cruise destinations for the wealthiest of passengers.

334 | RMS *Queen Elizabeth 2*, or *QE2* as she is familiarly known, in Sognefjord in the 1990s. Built on Clydebank and put into service in 1969, the flagship of the Cunard Line operated a regular transatlantic service between Southampton and New York. Converted into a troop carrier during the Falklands war of 1982, she was refitted in 1984 and again ten years later to accommodate 1800 passengers. Measuring 962.9 feet (293.5 meters) in length and with a beam of 105.1 feet (32 meters), she has a gross tonnage of 70,327. Taken out of service in November 2008, she is to be converted into a floating hotel in Dubai.

335 | At Gudvangen in Sognefjord, amenities were fairly basic, but small steamers could moor at the quay, as shown in this photograph taken in 1892.

336 | As the Hapag liner *Meteor* approaches the Hanseatic port of Bergen, two elegant lady passengers pose on the promenade deck as they await the arrival of the launch that will ferry them to shore. The first pier to accommodate cruise ships here was built only in 1917.

337 | The fish market in Bergen, the hub of this Norwegian town since the eleventh century, remains a very popular tourist attraction to this day.

338–339 | To round off a souvenir album of an Arctic cruise, this Belgian tourist has included a number of views of Copenhagen, the final port of call on this northern itinerary. At this time, Copenhagen was a very important port of transit.

340–41 | A Pacific Steamship Company advertisement showing the classic Alaskan cruise itinerary, featuring the famous Inside Passage.

342 | This double-funnel single-propeller steamer moored on the main jetty at Anacortes in Skagit County, Washington State, c. 1934, is the *Tacoma* of the Puget Sound Navigation Company. Launched in 1913 and taken out of service in 1935, she sailed between Seattle and Tacoma. Her maximum speed was 20 knots, and she was designed to accommodate a thousand passengers.

343 | The Inside Passage between Seattle and Ketchikan. The rugged beauty of this region attracted the attention of cruise lines very early on, and this route—one of the most beautiful in the world—is still very popular with cruise ships.

344 | A Pacific Steamship Company brochure from 1936 inviting tourists to discover Alaska by taking a cruise on a ship of the Admiral Line, along the "world's smoothest waterway."

345 | Passengers strike a pose on the quayside before embarking on an Alaskan cruise, c.1899.

346 | On August 5, 1910, while steaming at full speed in thick fog, the *Princess May* of the Canadian Pacific Railway Company ran aground on rocks off Sentinel Island, near the Lynn Canal. The lifeboats were launched immediately, and her 80 passengers and 68 crewmembers were all brought ashore safely—as was her cargo of gold. At low tide, the ship was left high and dry, as this photograph shows. A month later she was floated off by the Seattle tugboat Santa Cruz. Built in 1888, the little steamer carried on sailing until 1930, when she was scrapped.

347 | The clock says half past ten at night, but as this ship is in the Lynn Canal, at a latitude of 58° 69' 19"N, the sun has not set.

348 | In the 1930s, tourists followed in the tracks of the gold prospectors of the Klondike, their predecessors on the ships of the Alaska Steamship Company.

349 | "No matter whether you travel one-way between nearby ports of call, or take the longest cruise available, you will find the officers and personnel of the Alaska Line ever-anxious to make your trip a happy one . . . Ships of the Alaska Line offer you a real vacation home while you are sailing sheltered seas." From a 1930s brochure.

350 | The *Prince Rupert* of the Canadian Steamship Company sails past the Taku Glacier. Where the ice meets the sea it will break off under its own weight to form icebergs.

351 | The massive ice wall of the Hubbard Glacier dwarfs a small observation vessel, with passengers on board to admire the spectacle.

Hamburg-Amerika Linie

Nordlandfahrten

S.S. "ALBERTVILLE"

VINGT-TROISIÈME CROISIÈRE

Le Cap Nord et les Fjords de Norvège

du 10 août au 30 août 1935

DRIE-EN-TWINTIGSTE RONDVAART

De Noord Kaap en de Noorsche Fjorden

van 10 Augustus tot 30 Augustus 1935

En route pour le glacier

En contemplation
devant le glacier

L'Albertville
dans la baie de Svartissen

Arrivée à Svartissen vendredi
16 août à 6 heures.

326 Débarquement dans un lieu désert:
un petit baraquement où l'on achète
cartes du glacier et timbres-poste; le
long de la route petits marchands
de fleurs silencieux.
Promenade libre au glacier.

Svartissen est le nom d'un immense glacier
se trouvant sur le passage des paquebots
de croisières. C'est le seul glacier d'Europe
descendant jusqu'à la mer. Il couvre un
plateau d'environ 55 km de long sur 16 km
de large à une hauteur de 1200 m.

Le dernier canot quitte le quai de Svartissen à 11 h 30

DIPLÔM

Il est certifié pa
que M? Véry
passagers du vape
en voyage au
aujourd'hui a vi
CA
le point le plus se
NOR

Île des

Diner Norvégien

Suggestion du chef
du Camp lapon

Museaux de phoque   Pattes de goéland à l'escavèche

Pâté de foie de morue   Loup-phoque gratiné

❖

Hors cadre : Baleine, selon grosseur

❖

Méduses en belle vue

Spécialité laponne

❖

Cuisseau d'ours blanc, sauce boréale

ou

Contrefilet de renne à la daube

❖

Aileron de pingouin au riz polaire

❖

Glace du Pôle

❖

Banquises en tablettes

❖

Harengs confits

⚓

S.S. "ALBERTVILLE"   Samedi 17 Août 1935

327

HAPAG-NORDLANDFAHRTEN 1932

Ermäßigte Fahrpreise!

331

HAMBURG-AMERIKA LINIE · HAMBURG

332

2850. *Sogn*, Gudvangen.

Rich. Andvord, Eneret 1892.

338

Cour intérieure du
Château de Kronborg

Fontaine du
Château de Kronborg.

La petite nymphe du port

Château de Kronborg.

Les côtes suédoises à Elseneur.

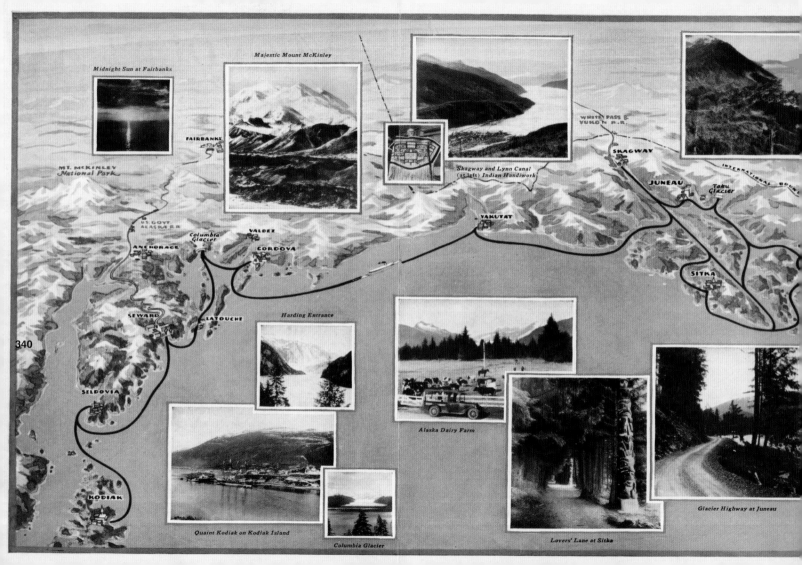

Midnight Sun at Fairbanks

Majestic Mount McKinley

Skagway and Lynn Canal
(at left) Indian Handiwork

MT. McKINLEY
National Park

FAIRBANKS

WHITE PASS &
YUKON R.R.

SKAGWAY

JUNEAU

INTERNATIONAL BOUND

Taku
Glacier

U.S. GOVT
ALASKA R.R.

Columbia
Glacier

VALDEZ

YAKUTAT

ANCHORAGE

CORDOVA

SITKA

340

SEWARD

LATOUCHE

Harding Entrance

Alaska Dairy Farm

SELDOVIA

KODIAK

Quaint Kodiak on Kodiak Island

Columbia Glacier

Lovers' Lane at Sitka

Glacier Highway at Juneau

(at left) Ketchikan on west coast of Revilla-gigedo Island

(below) Wrangell

(at left) Ketchikan Creek

(at left) Scene on Puget Sound

Cruising the
World's Smoothest Waterway
through the famous
INSIDE PASSAGE
and among the 10,000 islands of
ALASKA

THE ADMIRAL LINE
P.S.S.CO.

(at right) Mount Rainier near Seattle

Admiral Liner in Inside Passage

BURG
WRANGELL

KETCHIKAN

VANCOUVER

SEATTLE

VICTORIA

TACOMA

Tours Nos. 1 and 2 traverse the territory from Seattle to Skagway and Sitka—the Southern Alaska Summerland.
Tour No. 3 traverses the entire route from Seattle to Kodiak (but not including Skagway and Sitka.)
The routes of the steamships "Queen" and "Admiral Rogers" and the S.S. "Dorothy Alexander" differ slightly between Ketchikan, Skagway and Sitka and way ports as shown in itineraries.

Willard Cox

341

Cruising the
World's Smoothest Waterway
to ALASKA

Cruising the
World's Smoothest Waterway
to ALASKA

344

Pacific Steamship Co.

Pacific Steamship Co.

345

346

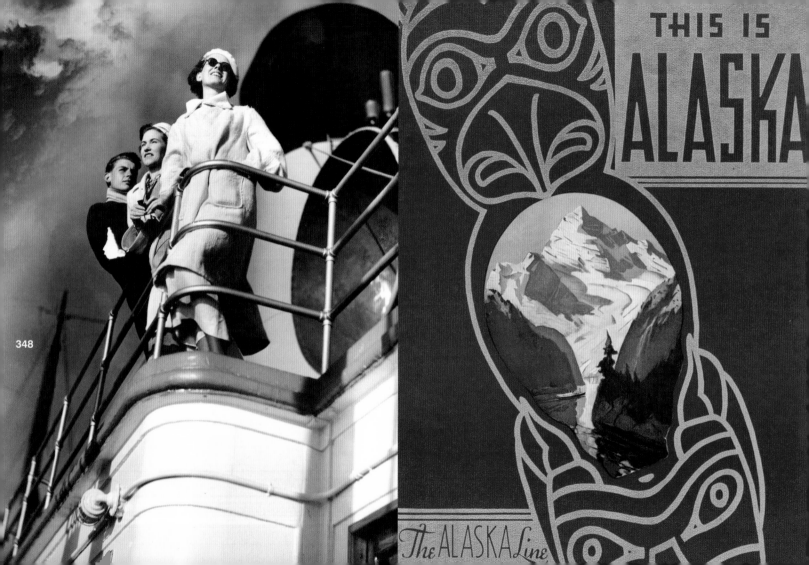

348

THIS IS
ALASKA

The ALASKA Line

350

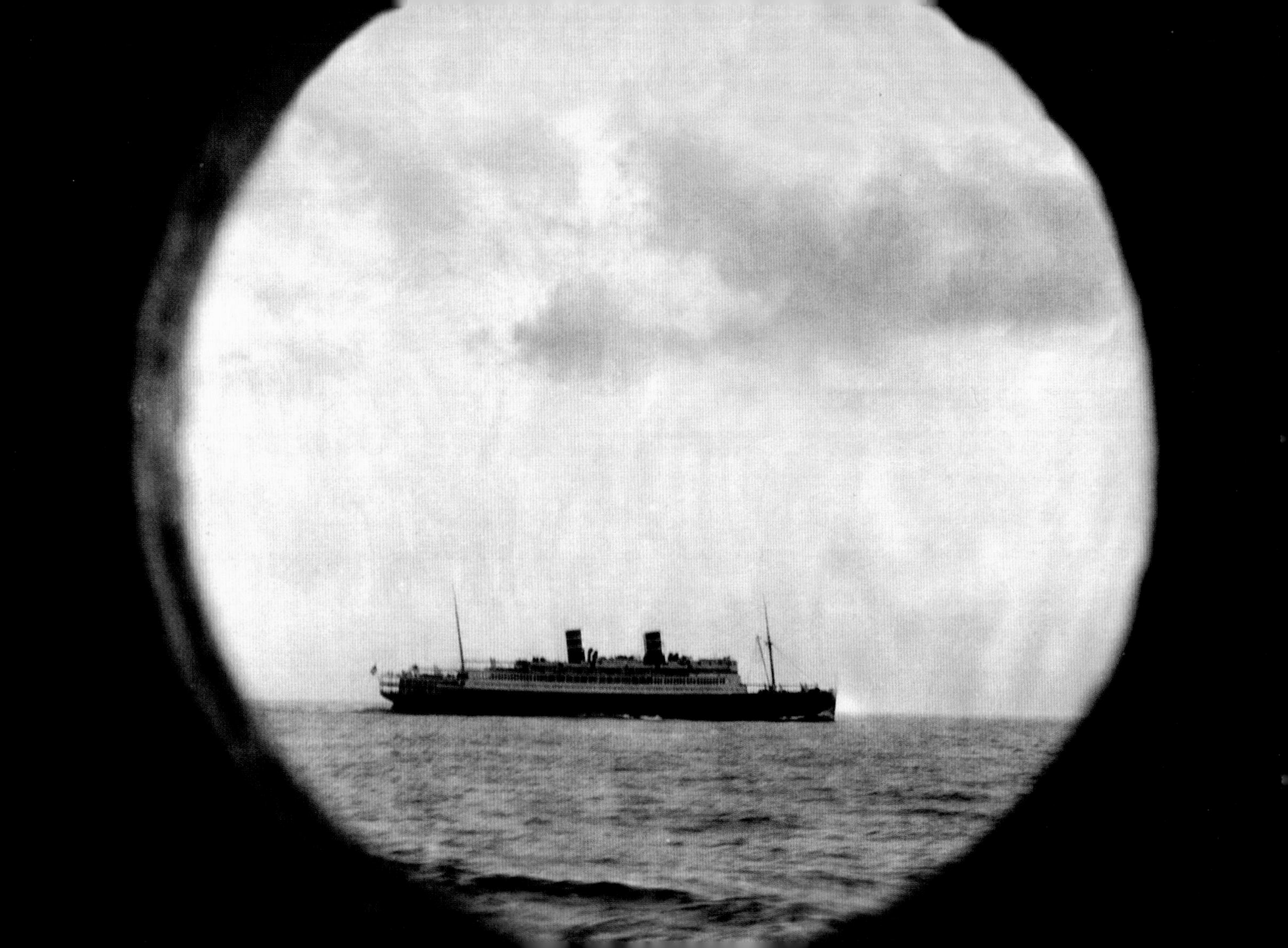

INDEX

Italic references denote illustrations.
A reference ending in "c" denotes a caption.

Abbazia, 64c, *87*
Acapulco, 265
Aden, 208, *211,* 212, 223c
Advent Bay, Spitzbergen, 319c, *325*
Africa, 155
Africa, 155
Aigle yacht, 51
air travel, effect on passenger shipping, 47, 60, 267, 314
Alameda, 308
Alaska, 310–313, 320c, *340–341*
Alaska, 313
Alaska Commercial Company, 308
Alaska Line, 320c, *349*
Alaska Steamship Company, *307,* 313, 320c, *348*
Albertville, 316, 319c, *326–327*
Alcock, Frederick, 156–161
Aleutian, 313
Alexandria, 64c, *94, 95,* 222c
Algiers, *48,* 63c, *70–71, 72, 73*
Alicante, *54,* 55c
Al Kahira, 222c
Allan Line, 16, 104
American Line, 29
American Mail Line, 262
American President Lines, 224c, 264, 265
Amerika, 19
Amérique, 112

Amiral de Kersaint, 224c, *249*
Amsterdam, 223c
Anacortes, Wash., 320c, *342*
Ancona yards, 33
André Lebon, 262
Andvord Bay, Neko Harbor, Antarctica, 168c, *198–199*
Annam, 223c
Antarctic, 317
Antilles, 167c, 168c, *184–185, 186*
Aquitaine, 63c
Aquitania, 26c, *31*
Arcadia, 265
Archimedes, 10
Arctic, 317
Arctic, 103
Ariadne, 38, 39c
Art Deco, 264
Art Nouveau, 59
Asama Maru, 264, 272c, *297*
Asie, 165c, *171*
Ateliers et Chantiers de Bretagne, 33
Athenic, 156
Atlantic, 102, 103c, 106
Atlantic Transport Line, 30
Atlantis, 62c, 63c, *68, 77*
Auckland, 265, 272c, *300*
Australia, 214
Australia, 272c, *301*
AZ Island concept (Zoppini), 47c, *47*

Bacardi, Facundo, 167c
Baedecker, Karl, 219
baggage, 34–37, *36–37,* 222c, *225*
Baltic, 101, 103

Baranof, 313
Bari, 55c
Barry, John Patrick, 62
Batavia, 214, 223c
Beirut, 64c, *92, 93*
Belawan, 222c
Bell, Jacob, 101c
Bemelmans, Ludwig, 116
Bergen, 314, 320c, *336, 337*
Bergensfjord, 314
Berlin, 120c, *145*
Bermuda, 167c, *175,* 265
Bird, Isabella, 270
Bismarck, 26
  renamed *Majestic,* 41
Black Bull Line, 9
Blohm & Voss, 33
Blücher, 316, 319c, *324*
Blue Riband contest, 42, 100, 112, 116
boarding, 36–39, 39c, *39*
Bombay (now Mumbai), 212, 222c, 223c, *236–237*
Boston Packets, 23
Brazza, 155
Bremen, 34
Bremen, 109, 115, 119c, 120c, *124, 144,* 314c, *315*
Bremer Vulkan-Vegesack, 33
Brindisi, 34, *203*
Britain
  imperial outreach of, 204
  shipbuilding yards, 33
  shipping lines, 19–26, 106
Britannia, 62c, *67, 99,* 100
Britannic (formerly *Gigantic*), 23, 29c, 41

British and American Steam Navigation Company, 99
British and North American Royal Mail Steam-Packet, 23, 100
British India Associated Steamers, 222c, *234*
Brunel, Isambard Kingdom, 10c, 13
Buenos Aires, *162,* 168c, *195*

Calcutta, 212c, *213,* 214, 223c, *241*
Callao, 260
Canada, shipping lines, 104
Canadian Pacific Line, 120c, 223c, 262–263
Cape Horn, 259
Cape of Good Hope, 204
Cape Town, 165c, *172–173*
Cardeza, Mrs. Charlotte, 34
Carinthia, 165c, *171*
Carlisle, Alexander, 19
Carmania, 16
Carnival Cruise Lines, 156
Carnival Destiny, 156
Cathay Pacific airline, 214
Central America, 155
Ceylon, 212
CGT. *See* Compagnie Générale Transatlantique
Champollion, 15, 57
Chargeurs Réunis, 59, 155, 158, 165c, 168c, *170, 190*
Cherbourg, 34, *38,* 39, 39c
Child's Glacier, Cordova, Alaska, 310c, *311*

Chile, 259
Chili, 156c, *156, 157,* 164
China Sea, 214
Churchill, Winston, 42
City of Brussels, 106
City of Panama, 271c
City of San Francisco, 271c
Clermont, 10, *10*
climate change, 317
coal, *210,* 211c, 263c
Coblenz, 14
Coffee, Frank, 267, 317
Collins Line, 101c, 103
Colombia, 271c
Colombie, 155–156
Colombo, 214, 222c, 223c, *238, 239*
Columbia Glacier, 313
Columbus, 120c, *138, 139, 152,* 155c
  renamed *Homeric,* 41
Compagnia di Navigazione Generale Italiana, 29, 164
Compagnie de Navigation Mixte, 53
Compagnie de Navigation Sud-Atlantique, *158*
Compagnie des Chargeurs Réunis, 26
Compagnie des Messageries Maritimes, 26, 42, 53, 63c, 158, 164, 168c, *195,* 204, 206, 214, 223c, 224c, *247, 251*
Compagnie Fraissinet Fabre, 26
Compagnie Générale Transatlantique (CGT) (French Line), 26, 41, 47,

51c, *51,* 53, 56, 104, 106, 112, 155–156, 158, 214, 319c
Compagnie Maritime Belge, 319c
Compagnie Paquet, 29, 52
Compañía Peruana de Vapores, 259
Compañía Sud-Americana de Vapores, 259
Compañía Trasatlántica Española, 29, 156
conferences (shipping), 207
Conrad, Joseph, *Lord Jim,* 208
Conway, Sir William Martin, 318
Cook, Thomas, 55
Copacabana beach, 168c, *192*
Copenhagen, 320c, *338–339*
Cordova, Alaska, 310c, *311,* 313
Corfu, 64c, *89*
Corinthic, 156
Coronel, 260
Corte Bianamano, 165c, *174*
Cromartyshire, 112, 119c
crossing the line (the equator), *160,* 161–162, 168c, *188, 189*
cruise ships, 47, 156, 168c, 316
Cuba, 167c, *180–181*
Cunard, Samuel, 100
Cunard Line, 19, 23, *23,* 26, 41, 42, 47, 56, *59,* 104c, *105*
  New York offices, *23*
Cyprus, 222c

Dakar, 165c
Davis, Arthur, 118
deck chairs, 272c, *285*
Det Nordenfjeldske Dampskibsselskab, 314
Deutschland, 27, 115
de Windt, Harry, 310
Dickens, Charles, 101, 119
disasters at sea, 103, 106, 112, 115, 119c, 164–165, 224c
Djibouti, 212

Dollar Steamship Company, 262, 263, 264, 272c
Dorothy Alexander, 308c, *309*
Drake Passage, 259
dress codes, 208c, *209,* 223c, *242*
Duilio, 28
Dunand, Jean, 120c
Duncan, Isadora, 64c
Dupas, Jean, 120c
Dutch East Indies, 223c

Ecuador, 260
Ecuador, 271c
Edinburgh, 314
Egypt, 55
  pyramids, *52,* 53c
El-Goléa, 53
Ellis Island, 120c, *151*
Elswick shipbuilding yard, 33
Empress of Australia, 167c, 168c, *176, 177, 178, 190*
Empress of Britain, 120c, *140–141*
Empress of Japan, 264
Empress of Russia, 272c, *296*
Empress of Scotland, 223c, *235, 271c, 282*
equator, crossing the, *160, 161–162,* 168c, *188, 189*
Eugène-Péreire, 17
Excelsior, 307, 308
Explorer, 165

Fairfield Shipbuilding and Engineering, 33
Far East, routes to, 203
Fastnet Rock Lighthouse, 106
Félix Roussel, 224c, *248*
ferrying passengers, 223c, *239*
Finnmarken, 316
Fitch, John, 10
Flandre, 167c, *184–185*
Florio company, 29
Forges et Chantiers de la Gironde, 33

Forges et Chantiers de la Méditerranée, 33
Foucauld, 155
Fram, 316–317
France
  imperial outreach of, 204
  shipbuilding yards, 33
  shipping lines, 26–29, 52–53, 104
France, 42c, *44–45,* 47
Franconia, 168c, *189*
freight trade of liners, 206–207
Fremantle, 265
French Line. *See* Compagnie Générale Transatlantique
Fulton, Robert, 10
funnels, markings on, 56–59
Furness Bermuda Line, 167c

G.A.P. Adventures, 165
Garnier, Edmond, 164
Gauguin, Paul, 221
Geiranger Fjord, *316*
Général Leclerc, 155
Genoa, 63c, *78–79*
Genoa yards, 33
George Philippar, 224c
Germany
  shipbuilding yards, 33
  shipping lines, 26, 106, 112
Gibraltar, 62c, *66,* 222c
glaciers, 319c, 320c
global warming, 317
Golden Gate, *256,* 259c
Gothic, 156
Gouverneur-type liners, 53
Gower, Lord Ronald, 221
Great Britain, 13
Great Eastern, 12, 13
Great Western, 11, 99–100
Great Western Steamship Company, 99–100
Greenland, 317
Guayaquil, 260
Gudvangen, 319c, *335*

Guion Line, 106
Gulf of Bengal, 214

Haines, 313
Haiphong, 224c, *249*
Hakodate, 262
Hales, Harold K., 100
Ha Long Bay, Vietnam, 224c, *246–247*
Hamburg, 34
Hamburg-Amerika Linie. *See* Hamburg-Amerikanische Packetfahrt Actien-Gesellschaft
Hamburg-Amerikanische Packetfahrt Actien-Gesellschaft (Hapag), 19, 26, 62c, 65, 104, 119c, 158, 167c, 174, 223c, 312, 313c, 314, 319c, 321, 331
Hamburg-Südamerikanische line, 42, 168c, *196*
Hammerfest, 313–314, 319c, *328*
Hanoi, 214
Hapag Line. *See* Hamburg-Amerikanische Packetfahrt Actien-Gesellschaft
Harland & Wolff shipbuilding yard, 19, 33
Havana, 158c, *159, 182–183*
Hawaii, 265–267, 272c
Heiyo Maru, 272c, *294–295*
Himalaya, 13, 222c, *228–229*
Hoboken, N.J., 120c, *150*
  Pier 2, *24–25*
Holland America Line, 271c
Hong Kong, 214, 214c, *215,* 224c, *251, 252, 253,* 262, 264, 272c, *294–295*
Honolulu, 262, 265
Horse Latitudes, 162
Hubbard Glacier, 320c, *351*
Hué, 214
hulls, metal, 10
Hurtigruten (Norway coastal express), 313–314, 316

Île-de-France, 41, 63c, *69*
immigration, 9, 9c, *9,* 120c, *137, 151,* 168c, 314
Impératice, 204
Imperator, 26, *26,* 39c, *96,* 99c, 119c, 120c, *135*
  renamed *Berengaria,* 41
India, 203, 212
Indian Ocean, 212
Indonesia, 223c
Indus, 223c
Industrial Revolution, 10
Inman Line, 106
Inside Passage, Alaska, 313, 320c, *340–341, 343*
interiors, 19
International Conference on the Safety of Life at Sea, 115
International Mercantile Marine (IMM), 29–30
International Navigation Company, 30
Isle of Wight, *104,* 106
Ismay, Thomas, 23
Istanbul, 64c, *90–91,* 222c
Italia Flotte Riunite (Italian Line), 42, 53, 56, 168c, *193*
Italy
  shipbuilding yards, 33
  shipping lines, 29, 53
  travel in, 55

Jaffa, *52*
Jakarta, 214, 223c
James, Henry, 103
Japan, 260–261
Java, 223c
Jeddah, 208
John Brown shipbuilding yard, 33
Jökulsárlón Bay, Iceland, 319c, *322*
J. P. Morgan and Company, 29
Juneau, 313
junk, Chinese, 224c, *251*

354

Kaiserin Auguste Victoria, 19,
119c, 132, 223c
Kaiser Wilhelm der Grosse, 108,
109c, 109, 110, 111, 112–115
Kaiser Wilhelm II, 20, 39c, 106c,
107
Karachi, 222c
Ketchikan, 313
Khedivial Mail Steamship &
Graving Dock Company,
222c
Kiendalsbreen Glacier, 319c,
333
kitchens, 14
Klondike gold rush, 307–310
Kobe, 262
Kodiak, 313
Kong Harald, 316
Kongsfjorden, Svalbard,
Spitzbergen, 319c, 323
König Albert, 18, 19c, 120c, 134
Korea, 264c, 265
Korean costumes, 272c, 299
Kosmos line, 158
Kotzebue, 313
Kraft durch Freude, 168c
Kristianiafjord, 314
Kronprinz Wilhelm, 21, 119c,
120c, 130, 138–139

Labouret, Auguste, 120c
La Bourgogne, 112, 119c,
122–123
La Bretagne, 112
La Hève, 106
La Joliette, 63c, 74, 222c,
226–227
Laos ships, 223c
Le Havre, 34, 265
Leonardo da Vinci, 10
Lesseps, Ferdinand de, 51, 222c,
271c
Leviathan (former Vaterland),
112c, 113c
Leyland Line, 30

lifeboats, 106c, 107, 164
Ligure Braziliana, 158
liners
building of, 30–34
conversion into troop carriers,
etc., 39–41, 42
Lisbon, 222c, 265
Liverpool, 119c, 121
Lloyd, William Whitelock, 13c,
222c
Lloyd Sabaudo, 165c
Loch Earn, 106, 106
Lofoten Islands, 319c, 330
Londres, Albert, 224c
Los Angeles, 265, 271c
The Love Boat, 267
Lucania, RMS, 22
Lurline, 272c, 293
Lusitania, 16, 16, 19, 23, 41, 41c,
41, 119c, 128
Lynn Canal, 320c, 347

Magdalena Fjord, Spitzbergen,
304, 307c
Magellan, 223c
mail steamers, 165c, 170
Malacca Straits, 214
Malta, 222c
Manchuria, 260
Manila, 262
Mann, Thomas, 60
Marghera yards, 33
Marseille, 222c, 226–227
Matsonia, 272c, 290–291
Matson Line, 263, 267, 271c,
272c, 287, 292
Maugham, W. Somerset, 217
Mauretania, 8, 9c, 16, 19, 23, 40,
41c
Mecca, pilgrimage to, 208
Mediterranean, 52
Meikong, 207
Melbourne, 265
merchant steamers, 56
Messageries Maritimes.

See Compagnie des
Messageries Maritimes
Meteor, 64c, 85, 320c, 336
Mewès, Charles, 19
Mexico, 155
Midnatsol, 316
midnight sun, 329, 347
Miller, James, 19
Mongolia (fictional ship), 203
Monte-class liners, 168c
Monte Sarmiento, 168c
Montevideo, 168c, 197
Montreal Ocean Steamship
Company, 104
Morgan, John Pierpont, 29–30
Mount McKinley, 313
Muggiano yards, 33
music rooms, 224c, 248

Nagasaki, 262
Naples, 34c, 35, 63c, 80, 81,
82–83
Nassau, 167c, 179, 265
National Line, 30
Navigazione Generale Italiana,
158
Nederland Line, 223c, 245
Neko Harbor, Antarctica, 168c,
198–199
Newcastle, 314
Newcomen, Thomas, 10
New-York and Havre Steamship
Navigation Company, 103
New York City, 39, 39c, 314
Niigata, 262
Nile, 55
Nippon Yusen Kaisha (NYK)
line, 207, 262, 272c, 296
Nomadic, 39
Norddeutscher Lloyd (NDL),
14c, 24–25, 104, 109, 112,
120c, 133, 158, 200, 203c,
207, 314
Nordkapp, 168c, 316
Nordkapp, Norway, 314–316,

319c, 329
Nordlys, 316
NordNorge, 165, 316
Normandie, 41–42, 116, 120c,
142, 143
Normannia, 63c, 73
North Atlantic crossing, 100
northeast passage, 317
Northern Star, 156
northwest passage, 317
Norway, 313–314, 319c, 331
Norwegian American Line, 314
Norwegian Caribbean Lines,
42c

Oceanic Steam Navigation
Company, 30
Olympic, 19, 19, 23, 29, 120c,
148–149
Oriana, 265
Orient Express, 55
Oropesa, 158–161, 162–164, 260,
261
Osaka, 262
Oslo, 314
Oslofjord, 314
Ost Afrika Linie, 42

Pacific, 103
Pacific Mail Steamship
Company, 263, 272c
Pacific Panama Line, 271c
Pacific Princess, 267
Pacific Steam Navigation
Company, 156–158, 259–260
Pacific Steamship Company,
320c, 340–341, 344
paddle wheels, 10
Pageot, Gaston, 260
Palermo, 56
Panama, 260
Panama Canal, 259, 263, 265,
271c, 276–277, 279, 280, 281,
282, 283
Panama Mail Steamship

Company, 271c, 278
Parsons, Sir Charles, 16
passengers
classes of, 16, 263
fun on ship, 176–178, 180–181,
190, 272c, 286
games on board ship, 223c,
243, 271c, 284
life on board ship, 222c, 223c,
228–229, 240
passenger trade
competition in, 207
effect of air travel on, 47, 60,
267, 314
Patria, 222c
Pears, Charles, 43c
Penfield, Frederic Courtland,
218
Peninsular & Oriental Steam
Navigation Company
(P&O), 23, 42, 56, 203–204,
206, 214, 222c, 223c, 242
Pereire brothers, 26
Peru, 260
Petersburg, 313
Peto, Harold, 19
Phileas Fogg (Jules Verne
character), 34, 203
Piraeus, 222c
P&O. See Peninsular & Oriental
Steam Navigation
Company
Poesia, 46, 47c
Polarlys, 316
Poppe, Johannes, 20c
Port Everglades, 265
Portland, 307
ports
linked to railways, 34
size of vessels
accommodated, 39
Port Said, 206, 211–212, 222c,
223c, 232, 233
President Cleveland, 265
President Coolidge, 264

355

President Hayes, 272c, *288–289*
President Hoover, 264
President Wilson, 224c, *250,* 265
Prince Rupert, 320c, *350*
Princess Cruises, 267
Princess May, 320c, *346*
Principessa Mafalda, 164, 165c, *169*
Prinzessin Victoria Luise, 63c, *72, 76*
Prohibition, 167c
propellers, 10, *32,* 33c
Puget Sound Navigation Company, 320c
Punta Arenas, 260

Queen Elizabeth 2, 47, 319c, *334*
Queen Mary, 34c, *34,* 42, 42c, *43,* 116, 120c, *146*
Queen Mary 2, 272c, *302–303*
Queenstown, 39

radio, 115c
Raftsund, 319c, *330*
railways, linked to ports, 34
Rangoon, 214
Real Ferdinando I, 63c
Red Sea, 222c
Red Star Line, 29–30
Ressel, Josef, 10
Rex, *114,* 115–116, 115c
Richard With, 316
Rio de Janeiro, 168c, *192*
Robert F. Stockton, 10
Roosevelt, Alice, 272c, *298*
Roosevelt, Theodore, 120c, *135*
Rotterdam Lloyd, 204, 222c, *230*
routes, safe, 106
Royal Mail Steamer (RMS), 13
Royal Mail Steam Packet Company, 26, 158
Rubattino company, 29
Ryndam, 271c, 272c, *292*

Sabang, 222c, 223c

safety, 112, 115
Saigon, 214
Saigon River, 223c
sailing ships, 63c, *78–79,* 204
St. George Steam Packet Company, 99
Sami family, *314*
Sandy Hook Lighthouse, 106
San Francisco, 260, 264, 265
San Francisco Bay, 260, 271c, *274*
Santos, 168c, *191*
Sauvage, Frédéric, 10
Scilly Isles, 106
Scotia, 104
seasickness, 161
Seattle, 262, *307*
Seldovia, 313
Seward, 313
SGTM. See Société Générale des Transports Maritimes
Shanghai, 214, 224c, *250,* 260, 262
Shaw Savill Line, 156
shipbuilding, 30–34
shuffleboard, *161*
Singapore, 214, *214,* 222c, 223c, *244*
Sirius, 99–100
Sitka, 308c, *309,* 313
Skagway, 313
smoking room, 165c, *171*
Société Générale des Transports Maritimes (SGTM), 29, 158
Société Maritime Nationale, 63c, *75*
Sognefjord, 319c, *334, 335*
Sonoma, 271c, *273*
South America, 155, 158
Southampton, 34, 119c, 222c
Southern Cross, 156
Spain
  shipping lines, 29, 156
  Spanish Civil War, 156
Spithead Naval Review of 1897,
16
Spitzbergen, 314, 319c, *323, 324*
Splendida, 32, 33c
Sri Lanka, 212, *212*
staircases, 19c
Star Cruises, 224c
Star Pisces, 224c, *253*
staterooms, 168c, *187,* 272c, *297*
Stavanger, 314
Stavangerfjord, 314
steam engine, 10, 99
steamships, 13
Stein, Gertrude, 117
Strait of Gibraltar, 155
Strait of Magellan, 259
study cruises, 62c, *68*
Suez, 208
Suez Canal, 51–52, 156, 203–205, 204c, *205, 207,* 222c, *231, 234, 235*
Suffren (former Blücher), 319c
Supphellebreen Glacier, 319c, *332*
Surabaya, 214, 222c, 223c
Svalbard, Spitzbergen, 319c, *323*
Swan Hunter & Wigham Richardson shipbuilding yard, 33
Sydney, Australia, 264, 265, *266,* 267c, 272c, *302–303*
Syria, 222c

Tacoma, 320c, *342*
Taft, William Howard, 272c, *298*
Taku Glacier, 320c, *350*
Tangier, 222c
Tanjung Priok, 223c
Tarabotto, Captain, 115–116
Tatsuta Maru, 264
tenders, 39
Tirard, Helen Mary, 61
Titanic, 19, 19c, 23, 29c, 115, 120c, 164–165
Tlingit girls, *310*
Toklas, Alice B., 117

Tokyo Bay, 272c, *296*
Tourane, 223c, *240*
Traffic, 39
Transat. See Compagnie Générale Transatlantique
transport ships, 264
Transylvania, 167c, *180–181, 182–183*
Trieste, 64c, *86*
Trollfjord, 316
Trondheim, 313–314
Turbinia, 16
Twain, Mark, 269

ukulele, 272c
Union Castle Line, 42
United Fruit Company (Great White Fleet), 167c, *177*
United States, 155
  shipping lines, 29–30
United States Lines, 41
Ushuaia, 317
US Steel, 29

Valdez, 313
Valetta, 223c
Valparaiso, *259*
Vancouver, 263, 265
Vaterland, 26, *30,* 119c, 120c, *129, 131, 150*
  renamed Leviathan, 41
Veloce, 158
Venezuela, 271c
Venice, *46,* 47c, 64c, *84, 85*
Vermont, 271c, *275*
Verne, Jules
  Around the World in Eighty Days, 34, 203, 220
  A Floating City, 13
  Propeller Island, 47
  The Purchase of the North Pole, 317
Vesteraalens Dampskibsselskap, 313
Vesterålen, 313–314

Vickers shipbuilding yard, 33
Victoria, 313
Victoria, B.C., 262
Victoria Luise, 53
Victorian, 16
Ville du Havre, 106, *106*
Villefranche-sur-Mer, 63c, *76*
Virginian, 16
Vulkan yards, 33

Wallace, David Foster, 166
warships, 56
Washington, 104
Watt, James, 10
Weser yards, 33
West Africa, 155
West Indies, 26, 155
White Star Line, 19, 19c, 23, *29,* 30, 41, 42, 106, 115, 164
Willamette, 308–310
With, Richard, 313
Witman, Bengt, 165
World War I, 39–41
World War II, 42, 264, 272c
Wrangell, 313

Yakutat, *310*
Yarrow shipbuilding yard, 33
Ybarra Line, 156
Yokohama, 214, *216,* 217, 224c, *254, 255,* 260–262, 272c, *298*
Yukon, 313

Zadar, 64c, *88*
Zoppini, Jean-Philippe, 47c

356

Citations

60 | Thomas Mann. *Death in Venice*. Translated by H. T. Lowe-Porter. New York: Random House, Vintage International, 1989, p. 19.

61 | Helen Mary Tirard. *Sketches from a Nile Steamer: For the Use of Travellers in Egypt*. London: Kegan Paul, Trench, Trübner & Co., Ltd., 1891, pp. 1–3.

62 | John Patrick Barry. *At the Gates of the East: A Book of Travel Among Historic Wonderlands*. New York: Longmans, Green, and Co., 1906, pp. 43–44.

116 | John Maxtone-Grahm. *The Only Way to Cross*. New York: Macmillan, 1972, p. 293.

117 Top | John Miller, ed. *San Francisco Stories: Great Writers on the City*. San Francisco: Chronicle Books, p. 96.

117 Bottom | Gertrude Stein. *A Stein Reader*. Evanston, IL: Northwestern University Press, 1993, p. 397.

118 | John Maxtone-Grahm. *The Only Way to Cross*. New York: Macmillan, 1972, pp. 112–117.

119 | Charles Dickens. *The Life and Adventures of Martin Chuzzlewit*. London: Chapman and Hall, 1866, Vol. 1, p. 268.

166 | David Foster Wallace. "Shipping Out: On the (nearly lethal) comforts of a luxury cruise." *Harper's Magazine*, January 1996, p. 48.

217 | W. Somerset Maugham. "P & O," *The Collected Short Stories*, New York: Penguin Classics, 1978, Vol. 4, p. 86.

218 | Frederic Courtland Penfield. *East of Suez: Ceylon, Indian, China and Japan*. New York: The Century, Co., 1907, pp. 10–12.

219 | Karl Baedecker, ed. *Egypt* Leipsic: Karl Baedecker, 1902, p.164.

220 | Jules Verne. *Around the World in Eighty Days*. Translated by Michael Glencross. New York: Penguin Putnam, 2004, p. 130.

221 Left | Lord Ronald Gower. *Notes of a Tour from Brindisi to Yokohama 1883–1884*. London: Kegan Paul, Trench & Co., pp. 42–43.

221 Right | Paul Gauguin. *The Writings of a Savage*. New York: Da Capo Press, 1996, p. 51.

267 | Frank Coffee. *Forty Years on the Pacific: The Lure of the Great Ocean*. New York: Oceanic Publishing Company, 1920, pp. 15–16.

268–69 | Mark Twain. *Following the Equator: A Journey Around the World*. New York: Harper & Brothers, 1906, Vol. 1, pp. 59–61.

270 | Isabella Bird. *The Hawaiian Archipelago: Six Months Amongst the Palm Groves, Coral Reefs, and Volacanoes of the Sandwich Islands*. London | John Murray, 1906, pp. 13–14.

317 | Frank Coffee. *Forty Years on the Pacific: The Lure of the Great Ocean*. New York: Oceanic Publishing Company, 1920, p. 237.

318 | Sir William Martin Conway. *The first crossing of Spitsbergen*. London: J. M. Dent & Co., 1897, p. 302.

Bibliography

Alcock, Frederick. *Trade & Travel in South America*. London: George Philip & Son, 1903.

Arqué, Sabine and Marc Walter. *Photochromie: Voyage en couleur, 1876–1914*. Editions Eyrolles, 2009.

Barber, James. *The Overland Guide Book*. London: Wm H. Allen and Co., 1815.

Battesti Michèle and Philippe Masson. *La Révolution maritime du XIXe siècle*. Paris: Editions Lavauzelle, 1987.

Le Livre de la Mer, various authors, Paris: Editions Larousse-Bordas, 1998.

The Cunard Steamship Company. London: Sutton Sharpe and Co., 1927.

Conrad, Joseph. *Lord Jim*. New York: Doubleday and Company, Inc., 1900.

Cotteau, Edmond. *En Océanie*. Paris: Librairie Hachette, 1888.

Crochet, Bernard and Gérard Piouffre. *Paquebots, des lignes réguli`res aux croisières*. Paris: Editions Du May, 2009.

De Windt, Harry. *Through the Gold Fields of Alaska to Bering Straits*. London: Chatto & Windus, 1898.

Dickens, Charles. *American Notes*. Cook Press, 2007 (Original publication 1842).

Donzel, Catherine. *Luxury Liners: Life On Board*. New York: The Vendome Press, 2006.

Ferrulli, Corrado, ed. *Au coeur des bateaux de légende*. Paris: Hachette Collections, 2004.

Fitzgerald, Percy. *The Great Canal at Suez*. London: Tinsley Brothers, 1876.

Filsinger, Ernst B. *Commercial Traveler's Guide to Latin America*. Washington: Government Printing Office 1920.

Garnier, Raymond. *Autour de monde*. Figuières, 1933.

Hale, Albert. *Practical Guide to Latin America*. Boston: Small, Maynard & Company Publishers, 1909.

Hériot, Madame. *Croisière en Méditerranée*. Coulommiers: P. Brodard, 1905.

James, Henry. *A Small Boy and Others*. New York: Charles Scribner's Sons, March 1913.

Lagier, Rosine. *Il y a un siècle, les paquebots transatlantiques*. Rennes: Editions Ouest-France, 2002.

Lawson, Will. *Steam in the Southern Pacific*. Wellington, New Zealand: Jackson and Co., 1909.

Lightoller, Charles Herbert. *Titanic and other Ships*. London: Ivor Nicholson & Watson, 1935.

Maddocks, Melvin. *The Great Liners*. Time-Life Editions, 1978.

Maginnis, Arthur J. *Atlantic Ferry*. London: Whittaker and Co., 1900.

McEwan, Robert D. *Zig-zagging Round the World*. London: Hutchinson & Co., 1922.

Pageot, Gaston. *A travers les pays jaunes*. Paris: Bibliothèque des auteurs modernes, 1908.

Pardieu, Comte Charles de. *Excursion en Orient*. Paris: Garnier Frères, 1851.

Piouffre, Gérard. *Dictionnaire de la Marine*. Paris: Editions Larousse, 2007.

———. *Le Titanic ne répond plus*. Paris: Editions Larousse, 2009.

Remy, Max. *Transatlantiques & long-courriers*. Rennes: Marines Edition, 1998.

Rentell, Philip. *White Star Liners*. Truro: Blue Water Publications, 1986.

Richardson, D.N. *A Girdle Round the Earth*. Chicago: A.C. McClurg and Company, 1888.

Rostron, Arthur H. *Home from the Sea*. London: Cassell & Company Ltd, 1931.

Seward, William Henry. *Voyage Around the World*. New York: D. Appelton & Co. 1873.

Short Lloyd, M. *Steamboat-Inspection Service*. New York: D. Appelton and Company 1922.

Siegfried, André. *Suez, Panama et les routes maritimes mondiales*. Paris: Librairie Armand Colin, 1940.

Wentworth Dilke, Sir Charles. *Greater Britain: A Record of Travel in English-Speaking Countries*. London: Macmillan and Co., 1907.

Photo Credits

v : Label
h : Top
b : Bottom
g : Left
d : Right

Alaska State Library / Skinner Foundation Photograph Collection : 348g (Rolphe Dauphin, p. 44-10-142), 349 (p. 44-10-008).
Andrea Valle / Dreamstime.com : 322.
Archives Association French Line, Le Havre, tous droits réservés French Line Diffusion : 15, 44-45 (photo M. Walter), 248 (photo M. Walter).
Bjorn Heller / Dreamstime.com : 334.
Canadian Pacific Archives, Montréal : 140-141.
Canada Science & Technology Museum, Ottawa : 350.
Celso Pupo Rodrigues/Dreamstime.com : 172-173.
Chambre de Commerce et d'Industrie de Cherbourg Cotentin (photo M. Walter) : 38.
Chris Lund/National Film Board/Library and Archives Canada/PA-152023 : 136.
Christian Mueringer / Dreamstime.com : 253.
Coll part : 2, 26, 27,146, 158, 190d, 196, 200, 230, 251g.
Cunard Archive, University of Liverpool : 31.
Deutsches Schiffahrtsmuseum,

Bremerhaven : 14, 144, 160, 315.
Formasia : 294-295.
Garret Bautista / Dreamstime.com : 351.
Library of Congress Prints and Photographs Division, Washington : 4, 9, 12, 16, 19, 23h, 24-25, 29, 30, 37, 39h, 39b, 40, 41, 70-71, 96, 99, 101, 102, 105, 106, 107, 109v, 113, 115, 124g, 125, 128, 129, 131, 132, 135, 137, 147d, 148-149, 150, 151, 162, 210, 215, 231, 232, 252, 259, 262, 265, 298, 299, 308, 310, 311, 342, 342v, 345, 346.
Michel Van Loon / Dreamstime.com : 256.
MSC Crociere : 32, 46.
National Libray of Australia, Cambera / Hurley negative collection / nla.pic-an23477971/ PIC PIC FH/412 LOC Cold store PIC HURL 26/17 : 266 (Franck Hurley).
Petesmile / English Wikipedia : 302-303.
San Francisco Maritime National Historical Park : 273, 293.
Steve Estvanik/Dreamstime.com : 198-199, 347.
Sidney D. Gamble Photographs, Archive of Documentary Arts, Duke University : 274, 283, 284, 285, 286.
Terence Mendoza / Dreamstime.com : 343.
The Royal Society of Marine Artists, courtesy of the National Maritime Museum : 43 (Charles Pears).
Tom Dowd / Dreamstime.com : 276-277.
UK National Archives, Crown Copyright : 67.

Vérascopes-Richard/Photothèque Hachette : 209, 275 (Domange).
Walter, Marc : 81, 84.
Walter, Gaspar : 246-247.
Walter (Collection) : 1, 6-7, 8, 10, 11, 13 (© P&O), 14v, 17, 18, 20, 21, 22, 23v, 28, 29v, 34, 35, 36v, 48, 51, 52h, 52b, 53, 54, 55, 56, 57, 58, 59, 65, 66, 68g, 68d, 69, 72, 73, 74, 75g, 75d, 76, 77, 78-79, 80, 82-83, 85, 86, 87, 88, 89, 90-91, 92, 93, 94, 95, 104, 108, 109, 110, 111, 114, 121, 122-123, 124d, 126-127, 130, 133, 134, 138g, 138-139, 139d, 142, 143, 145, 146v, 152, 155, 156, 157, 159, 160v, 161, 163, 169, 170, 171, 171v, 174g, 174d, 175, 176, 177, 178, 179, 180-181, 182, 183, 184-185, 186, 187, 188, 189, 190g, 191, 192, 193, 194, 195, 197, 203, 205, 206, 207, 211, 212, 213, 214h, 214b, 225 (© P&O), 226-227, 228-229 (© P&O), 233, 234, 235, 236-237, 238, 239, 240, 241, 242g, 242v, 242d (© P&O), 243, 244, 245, 247d, 249, 250, 251d, 252, 254, 255, 261, 262v, 263, 267, 278, 279, 280, 281, 282, 283v, 287, 287v, 288-289, 290-291, 292g, 292d, 296, 296v, 297, 300, 301, 304, 307, 309, 312, 314, 316, 321, 323, 324, 325, 326-327, 328, 329, 330, 331, 332, 333, 335, 336, 337, 338, 339, 340-341, 344, 348g, 352.
Zoppini, Jean-Philippe : 47.

Acknowledgments

The author would like to express his thanks to the following individuals for their help and for the information they have supplied: Mme Catherine Donzel, travel historian; Mlles Nadine Cherubini and Anne-Aymone Rossin, historians of the *Titanic*; M. Arnaud Prudhomme, military historian; Mr. Clive Lamming, railway historian; and Mr. Bernard Crochet, historian of the Industrial Revolution. He is particularly indebted to M. Raphaël Gérard, director of exhibitions for the Direction du Patrimoine et des Etablissements Louis Vuitton Malletier, who kindly gave permission for the reproduction of photographs of two vintage traveling trunks.

And there's no cure like travel
To help you unravel
The worry of living today.
When the poor brain is cracking
There's nothing like packing
A suitcase and sailing away.

CODE PORTER,
"Bon Voyage" from *Anything Goes,* 1934

Front cover | The arrival in New York harbor of the SS *France*, the world's longest passenger ship, on her maiden voyage in February 1962.

First published in the United States of America by The Vendome Press, 1334 York Avenue, New York, N.Y. 10021
www.vendomepress.com

Copyright © Editions du Chêne-Hachette-Livres 2009
Translation copyright © The Vendome Press 2009

Translation: Barbara Mellor
U.S. edition editor: Sarah Davis

Series concept and artistic direction: Marc Walter / Chine
Design: Florence Cailly / Chine
Cartography: Emilie Boismoreau / Chine
Editor & picture researcher: Boris Dänzer-Kantof / Chine
Additional material: Catherine Donzel / Chine
Photogravure: Planète Graphique

Library of Congress Cataloging-in-Publication Data

Piouffre, Gérard.
First class : legendary ocean liner voyages around the world / text by Gerard Piouffre.
p. cm.
ISBN 978-0-86565-256-9
1. Ocean travel. I. Title.
G550.P58 2009
910.4'5—dc22
2009020158

Printed in China by SNP Leefung
First printing